THE SIMPLE LIFE GUIDE TO SMALL HABITS FOR BIG CHANGE

14 Powerful Lessons for Living a Life of Success and Integrity

GARY COLLINS, MS

THE
SIMPLE
LIFE

The Simple Life Series (Book 5)

The Simple Life Guide To Small Habits For Big Change: 14 Powerful Lessons for Living a Life of Success and Integrity

(First Edition)

Printed in the United States of America

Copyright ©2020

Published by Second Nature Publishing, Albuquerque, NM 87109

For information about special discounts for bulk purchasing, and/or direct inquiries about copyright, permission, reproduction and publishing inquiries, please contact Book Publishing Company at 888-260-8458.

DISCLAIMER OF WARRANTY

The intent of this material is to educate you in the area of self-improvement.

The text and other related materials are for informational purposes only. The data, author's opinions, and information contained herein are based upon information from various published and unpublished sources that represent self-improvement and practice summarized by the author and publisher. Even though the author has been as thorough as possible in his research, the publisher of this text makes no warranties, expressed or implied, regarding the currency, completeness, or scientific accuracy of this information, nor does it warrant the fitness of the information for any particular purpose. Any claims or presentations regarding any specific products or brand names are strictly the responsibility of the product owners or manufacturers. This summary of information from unpublished sources, books, research journals, articles, and the author's opinions are not intended to replace the advice or recommendations by professionals.

Due to the great variability of self-improvement, and so forth, the author and Second Nature Publishing assume no responsibility for personal injury, property damage, or loss from actions inspired by information in this book.

TABLE OF CONTENTS

GET YOUR FREE GOODIES

Get Your Free Goodies and Be a Part of My Special Community!

Building a solid relationship with my readers is incredibly important to me. It's one of the rewards of being a writer. From time to time, I send out an email to what I call "The Simple Life Insider's Circle" (never spammy, I promise) to keep you up to date with special offers and information about anything new I may be doing. I've moved away from using social media in the pursuit of a simpler life, so if you want to be part of the "in crowd," The Simple Life Insider's Circle is the place to be.

If that's not enough enticement, when you sign up, I'll send you some spectacular free stuff!

- **The Five Simple Life Success Principles printout.**
- **How to identify and rid yourself of bad habits printout.**
- **Gary's simple and quick how-to meditate technique.**

- **Free chapter from *The Simple Life - Life Balance Reboot* book.**
- **10% off and free shipping on your first order at The Simple Life website.**

You'll get these goodies when you sign up to be a part of The Simple Life Insider's Circle at:

http://www.thesimplelifenow.com/14Habits

OTHER BOOKS BY GARY COLLINS

The Simple Life – Life Balance Reboot: The Three-Legged Stool for Health, Wealth and Purpose

The Simple Life Guide To Financial Freedom: Free Yourself from the Chains of Debt and Find Financial Peace

The Simple Life Guide To Decluttering Your Life: The How-To Book of Doing More with Less and Focusing on the Things That Matter

The Simple Life Guide To Optimal Health: How to Get Healthy and Feel Better Than Ever

The Simple Life Guide To RV Living: The Road to Freedom and The Mobile Lifestyle Revolution

The Beginners Guide To Living Off The Grid: The DIY Workbook for Living the Life You Want

Living Off The Grid: What to Expect While Living the Life of Ultimate Freedom and Tranquility

Going Off The Grid: The How-To Book of Simple Living and Happiness

Consulted and Co-Authored by Gary Collins - The Crime Beat Thriller Series by Best Selling Author AC Fuller

DEDICATION

I have never done a book dedication before, and probably will never do one again. But considering the driving theme of this book (which I'll reveal later) and after the recent passing of Neil Peart, the lyricist and drummer of my favorite band Rush, I felt this was something I had to do. Even if you are not a Rush fan, you would be surprised by how many musicians, actors, politicians, writers/creators, bastions of freedom, and just the average every day person, have been influenced by their music and lyrics. I happen to fit several of those above categories, including being a die-hard Rush fan for over forty years. I will take it a step further... Rush has been my number-one favorite band for nearly my entire life. There isn't really a close second! That is the thing about Rush fans—we consider ourselves part of a family, because being a Rush fan is much more than just liking their music. I believe this is because Rush lived and worked by the simple idea you'll be learning about in this book.

I consider myself incredibly lucky to have been alive during Rush's career. There are many reasons for this, but here are a few that stick out. First, the members of Rush are best friends, and have been during most of their lives. Geddy Lee, the singer and bassist, and Alex Lifeson, the guitarist, met in junior high. How many bands can say that? Second, Rush is the hardest working band that has ever existed, and they have never conformed to what record companies thought they should be. Third, they take their craft incredibly serious and are the utmost professionals, not only in their craft, but also as people.

This will sound crazy to most, but I don't think I would be the person I am today without Rush's influence. Matter of fact, just an hour before they announced Neil's passing, I had included a lyric from one of their songs to prove one of my points in this book. Again, something I had never done before. I definitely feel that not only this book, but many of my other books, are directly influenced by Rush. And I'm not the only one who will say this. They have touched so many people during their career. They have motivated many of us to live the life we want, but also, to be the best people we can be and to be thankful for everything we have.

A couple of Rush's songs resonated with me greatly growing up. But it would be difficult for me to say I have a couple definitive favorite songs. For example, the lyrics in "Subdivisions" (from the album *Signals* - 1982), and "Emotion Detector" (from the album *Power Windows* - 1985), which are very different albums from each other. Considering these albums were released during my teenage years, while I was shaping my beliefs and figuring out who I was, it is no surprise that Rush's most influential songs for me came from this period.

"Subdivisions" is about the urban sprawl and teen angst of the 70s and 80s in North America. The lyrics of this song echo what a lot of young people were thinking at the time—not fitting into what society told us we should be…

Growing up it all seems so one-sided
Opinions all provided
The future pre-decided

Detached and subdivided
In the mass production zone
Nowhere is the dreamer
Or the misfit so alone

I think many of us growing up during this time felt that our identity and Free Will were being eroded away. We were expected to conform, and we were struggling with this. Matter of fact, I still struggle with this today. But I've also learned that fitting in isn't nearly as important as living a life true to yourself. The fact that you're reading this tells me you're starting to realize this too. That's why this book is based on the simple idea of living with personal integrity. And I'm not just talking about integrity as in "doing the right thing." Heck, even terrorists believe they're doing the right thing. I'm talking about living a life true to your principles instead of living by someone else's rules. Rush's music introduced me to this idea, and today I see it as the ONLY path to inner peace and happiness. That's why I've based this book on that simple idea.

Another Rush song, "Emotion Detector" came out at the most pivotal time in my young life. Because of a tragic, life altering event, 1985 would be the last time I spoke with my father. I'm not comfortable sharing all the details of this event just yet. But I remember sitting on my bed with tears in my eyes listening to the words of "Emotion Detector"...

When we lift the covers from our feelings
We expose our insecure spots
Trust is just as rare as devotion —
Forgive us our cynical thoughts
If we need too much attention —
Not content with being cool
We must throw ourselves wide open
And start acting like a fool

If we need too much approval
Then the cuts can seem too cruel

This is probably the most sensitive information I have ever shared about my personal life. It relates to the trials and tribulations of what shaped me into the person I am today. Rush has always been a very private band, so I guess that rubbed off on me a bit as well. I have never looked for sympathy or for the spotlight to shine on me in anything I've done. It's always been about the message.

It is amazing to me that songs written in 1982 and 1985 are still just as powerful and relevant today. That is the genius of Rush. They didn't write about getting laid, partying like... well, like rock stars. Their songs were very deep, not only musically, but lyrically unique. Neil tackled the deep psychological aspects of life and being human in this crazy world. No other band has played the type of music (cerebral yet melodic) with accompanying lyrics that made you think.

When you had those lyrics in front of you, you felt they were speaking directly to you. It was as if they understood what you were thinking and going through. As a "want to be guitar player" since the age of fifteen, their music was just mind blowing to me. No band has ever come close to their level of musicianship, and they did it with only three members.

Since their retirement in 2015, which I was lucky enough to see two shows on that tour, I had hoped that just maybe they would get together one more time. Now I know that is not going to happen. But I have over four decades of the best music and memories a fan could ever ask for.

All that said, I want to thank Rush for being Rush. I especially want to thank Neil for being a champion of hope and integrity and of overcoming incredible hardships in life. I highly recommend you read his book *Ghost Rider*, which is one of the best books I have ever read about dealing with tragedy and finding redemption. For those of you who do not know, in the late 1990s, Neil's nineteen-year-old daughter was killed in a car accident. Ten months later his wife succumbed to cancer. Again, Rush is much more than just a band. They teach us about perseverance, and about doing the right thing, even when it is not popular and even if it's not in our best interest. This is what it means to live your life by principles instead of being ramrodded by someone else's agenda. This is personal integrity, and it's the only path to true inner peace and happiness. We'll talk about these principles and their accompanying Habits in this book.

Rest in peace Neil, even though you are gone I will continue to follow your *Vapor Trails*.

GUESS WHAT? I'M NOT SUPPOSED TO BE HERE!

If I had followed the road, I was destined to be on; I would not be where I am today. A pretty bold statement, right? As some may know, my childhood was not one of the best, but you know what? That is the case for a great many people. You can cry and whine about it, or you can dust yourself off and move on. Playing the victim is never the right way to go. If I would have followed that path, which is what society, and a lot of people expected me to do. I would probably be living in a beat-up trailer, maybe even sitting in a prison cell, and/or an extensive criminal history, collecting some sort of public assistance, with drug and alcohol issues… or worse like a lot of people I grew up with and family members—dead!

Simply put, the Habits in this book saved my life.

Very early on, I started in a middle-class family… then after my dad succumbed to several bad life decisions and his battle with addiction—from there on, it was "Poorville." After my parents divorced, I lived in the spare "bedroom" of a converted single-wide trailer with my mom and stepdad. One of the numerous "Redneck Engineers" had slapped a "wall" and roof over the trailer's outside deck and cut a hole in for my bedroom door. So, I slept in the same room with the hot water heater and an inside facing "window" that was once our *outside-facing* bathroom window. This room was so poorly insulated, I could literally see my breath during the winter. Since we couldn't afford me running a space heater, I remember crawling under an electric blanket, head and all, to avoid freezing my ass off. In the summer, I had a free sauna!

Worse yet, rain would leak through the roof and into my room. When this happened, my room was a maze of cups and small buckets. But you know what? That's how EVERYTHING worked in my family. Everything was half-assed to "save" time and money, and we just dealt with the shitty conditions that followed. Everything was about cutting corners.

Looking back, I could have easily used all this as an excuse to half-ass my way through life and blame everyone when my life turned out to suck because of it. That was the path I was destined to follow. Then one day, when I was fourteen years old, after weeks of sitting in my room getting rained on, I grabbed some tools, climbed onto our roof, and found the leaky spots above my "bedroom." I took my time fixing them. I knew that if I didn't, I would have to get rained on, again... and wait for a sunny day, again... then climb back up on the roof, again... and try to make up for doing a half-ass job the first time. So I summoned my inner perfectionist and did the best job I could. No more leaks.

That's the day I started learning that shortcuts just make everything harder, messier, and more complicated. While I didn't fully understand the concept of integrity back then, I began to realize that there's tremendous satisfaction, peace, and happiness in doing things right the first time. But that didn't mean things got instantly better.

Then I was fifteen years old, my dad committed a horrific

crime, which resulted in him spending several years in prison. His life-long path of making poor decisions and blaming others had finally caught up with him—big time. I decided he was a toxic person, and I could allow him to influence me negatively, or I could move on. I decided to move on. I never spoke to him again, even up to his death. Some may say that is cruel, but I'll tell you right now, that was me again exercising my Free Will, and I have never regretted it... not once!

To this day, I've never been so naïve as to assume I couldn't have ended up there myself if I hadn't watched the people around me sink themselves into mediocrity and failure by taking shortcuts. Today, nearly forty years after that day on the roof, I've learned that if I can live my purpose, anyone can create a damn good life simply by choosing the right habits and by living with integrity.

I've been asked over the years, what kept me off the road predestined for me, and what makes me so tenacious at living the best life I can? The answer is simple. As you see above, I recognized the mistakes my friends and family were making growing up, and I decided early on—I don't have to be like them. I'm not saying I'm perfect and walk around with a golden halo, but I give it my best every day to learn from my upbringing and live a life of integrity. Sometimes I fail, but I don't give up. Nothing has ever come easy for me in life. I'm a grinder. There are no 100 million-dollar podcast deals knocking at my door, book publishing companies offering me contracts to set me up for life, or anyone just looking to throw this dog a bone. It never has or does work out that way for me.

Yet again, that is how it is for a lot of people. Yes, even very successful people. The thing in common we all have is we work on positive habits... continuously! There are many roads in life you can take. It is up to you to choose your own path. You can blame others for the outcomes in your life, or you can get out there and make it happen. Like my story, they aren't sexy because they show the ugly, the grinding day after day, and most importantly—the failures. Those cute and sparkly success stories are usually made up, which is very common in the self-help world, or they leave out all their failures.

Just because life has paved a trail for me to end up in a ditch doesn't mean I have to follow it. And you know what? If I end up in the ditch, I can assure you in almost all cases; it is my fault... so I'm the one who needs to get myself out of it. That is the attitude I have carried with me in life, and it has never let me down.

Here's the thing—I know that life isn't going to make things easy on you, but that's okay. With the right habits, you can free yourself from the shortcut chasing mindset, learn good habits, discover your purpose, and go on to make it real. If your early life paved a trail for you to end up in a ditch, we have that in common. It has forced me to integrate my habits with my values and to live by what I teach others. That's how I know these habits can change your life.

I hope after reading this book, you will realize that I'm no one special. I'm going to say things in this book that piss you off, and I don't blame you for that. No one likes to admit that their habits need to change. But, I hope my story shows you that I do this from a place of deep respect for your natural-born power to choose your own path and out of a desire to help you in the best way I can. No matter what your life has been like up to now. You can choose to make it better. I know this because I wasn't born with a silver spoon up my butt. Chances are, you and I have that in common, and if I can do this, so can you, maybe even better.

INTRODUCTION - WHAT IS THIS BOOK ABOUT?

I'm going to do something a little unorthodox. I'm going to start by telling you what this book is **NOT** about. Trust me, as I introduce you to The Simple Life Philosophy you will understand why I did it this way.

First, this will not be not some rah-rah book written by someone whose only claim to fame is calling themselves a "self-help" or "motivational" expert. That's exactly what you'll find when you look into the background of most self-help authors, which I highly encourage you to do. Such authors are what I call the "False Prophets" of the self-help world. They are simply pretenders who have, in most cases, teamed up with or learned their schtick from other self-acclaimed self-help "experts." I will tell you this firsthand as a former investigator, most self-help people are completely full of shit! I have read enough of their nonsense over the years and decided I have had enough—so should you. Again, look into their backgrounds and you'll see what I'm talking about.

How many times have we heard that an author's claim to fame came very early on in their life, before they even knew what the hell life was about? They'll tell you they started out selling some useless overpriced widget door to door. And, of course they were just the most amazing door to door salesman ever to exist! Or maybe they were in a life altering car accident. Or, better yet their parents stopped paying for their college, which changed their life and made them experts in how to lead the rest of us to success. Boohoo for them, right? Again, these stories usually came early on in the author's life. Before they had any shred of real-life experience. And now, they want to tell you how to overcome life's most difficult obstacles? Many of which they've never faced themselves? I smell bullshit!

Don't misunderstand me. There are some very good self-help authors and books out there. But I have found ninety-nine-percent of them to be completely useless for anything more than putting money in the author's pocket. My mission is to fix that by writing and publishing the kind of self-help books I wish I'd had thirty years ago.

BEING AUTHENTIC BEATS BEING ENTERTAINING

The second thing you should know about me is that I'm a real person. I don't sugar coat things. I go on rants. I use profanity from time to time. I have been trying to get better about that over the years. But having spent half my life in military intelligence and as a special agent, it is a hard (bad) Habit to break. But here is the difference between me and some other "Shock Jock" authors: I don't do this for shock and awe. The use of occasional profanity is a part of how I feel and speak. If I censor myself on that point, I'm no longer being authentic and would have no business writing a book about the topic. That said, I don't publish books with "fuck" on the cover and sprayed thousands of times throughout the text, just to prove that I'm a bad ass. Honestly, that is pure psychological warfare from the False Prophets. It's a way to rattle your brain, and to distract you with shocking language so you won't realize that the author, in most cases, has no clue what they are talking about. How many books or blogs are out there now with some curse word in the title, all designed to make you go clickety click...

"I must have that"?

It reminds me of the scene in Forest Gump, where Tom Hanks' character sees a political activist giving a speech and says:

"There was a man giving a speech. And he liked to say the "F" word... A lot. F this and F that. And every time he said the "F" word, people, for some reason, well, they cheered."

Shocking language might be entertaining. But it can also distract people into thinking that there's more substance to what you're saying than there really is. For the love of God stop with it already!

So, I'm not here to shock and awe you. I'm here to help you find a positive proactive path in life. The path you want. Not the path society, or some False Prophet has told you that you must follow. But I'm not afraid to be raw and real about what it takes to do that. As I said in my dedication, living with personal integrity isn't about conforming to someone else's rules about how you should behave. It's not about trying to look good for others. It's about having one set of rock-solid Principles AND Habits upon which to base your consistent actions. Most importantly, it's about resting your head on your pillow at night with the assurance that you're not having to look over your shoulder and see if someone is onto you. This book gives you the Principles and Habits to make this possible.

THERE'S NO SUBSTITUTE FOR EXPERIENCE

The most important thing you should know about me is that I have a simple philosophy when it comes to teaching and helping people. First, you need to have your act together before you start helping others. This is one of the key factors the False Prophets are great at... do as I say, not as I do. Many of them talk about things they know nothing about, as if they're experts in the subject, and yet they get away with it.

For example, I'm amazed at how many people try to get their health on track by following people who are in just as bad or worse shape than them. I call this the "Oprah Winfrey Effect." Millions and millions of people have followed and bought Oprah Winfrey's health products. This has made Oprah even richer. Which she really didn't need. But I question how much it's really helped the people buying her stuff.

I say this because Oprah is a billionaire with all the resources known to humankind. Yet, she constantly struggles with her weight and her health. Why in the world would you get your health advice or purchase health products from someone like this? If you want to get advice on how to create a media empire you might want to listen to her. But when it comes to weight-loss and how to live a healthy life, it makes zero sense to go to Oprah for advice.

Oh, and I can already hear it...

"Gary, you're fat shaming Oprah, and everyone who is struggling with their health!"

If you honestly think this way, this book is not for you. You might want to try a romance novel instead. Following the False Prophets is one of the biggest problems people face today (all self-imposed I may add). And when their miracle product doesn't work, guess what they have next... another miracle product!

The second part of my Simple Life Philosophy is that if you want to help people and teach them, you need what I call *"butt in the seat and time in the salt mines experience."* This is my common sense take on knowledge and experience as it relates to teaching others. This is nothing against young and aggressive want-to-be life motivators. But if you haven't mastered the above, you in no way should be telling others how to live their life. No matter how smart you think you are or how much you care. Hell, look at all the time, money, and energy doctors invest into themselves before they can even advertise and start seeing patients. If you're not willing to pay that kind of price to become a self-help expert, I question whether you're doing this for anything more than fame and profits.

This is why I firmly believe no one should ever write a self-help book in their twenties. No matter what they have gone through. I went through some devastating stuff when I was that age. But at no point in my younger years did I think I had the knowledge and experience to guide people on some of their most critical life choices. Especially not people who had more years in their life and more life in their years than I had. That may be just my take on it. But I think you should consider this before you purchase your next self-help book from that trendy, charismatic twenty-something hotshot.

Yes, I went on a tangent a bit. But these are critical factors you must think about when trying to change your life for the better. I have found no one will bring these critical points to the surface. They're too worried about offending people. Well I'm NOT. Soft corners and flattery won't help anyone get better. The proof is in the pudding. For example, we are the most obese we have ever been in the United States, and it is getting worse at an alarming rate. We are more depressed than we were ten years ago. We have an epidemic of addiction and of just flat out not being happy. Yet, we have more self-help information at our fingertips than any society in history.

So why keep doing what we're doing and reading what we're reading when it's clearly not working? That is what The Simple Life is all about—finding and implementing the things that work. It's not about taking the easy road, which usually leads to nowhere. It's not about being seduced by shocking or entertaining language and by charismatic personalities. It's about integrating your Habits with bedrock principles that produce real results. That's what it means to live with personal integrity.

To sum this up, I have a saying when it comes to how I teach The Simple Life Philosophy:

"If you are looking to chase butterflies, ride unicorns and pet bunny rabbits this is probably not the place for you."

If you're still reading, I'm guessing you're not one of these people.

SO, WHAT IS THIS BOOK ABOUT?

Now that I've weeded out all the Self-Help Tourists, what is this book about? It is pretty simple. It's about developing and changing your Habits so that you can live a successful and happy life. The key to living with integrity is to have a simple set of Principles and Habits to live by. The simpler you make things, the less you have to rely on willpower or overthinking to keep up with your plans. More importantly, simplicity means you don't have to constantly worry about whether you're checking all the boxes on some stupid system. This is the simple secret to a successful and happy life.

Yes, that last sentence is a loaded statement that demands some concrete explanation. We'll get to that. For now, let me just say that happiness is what we all want. We also want peace of mind, and we want to feel like our life matters. We just need the right information to help us achieve these things. We are flooded with so much bullshit today and it is getting harder and harder to decipher the good from the bad.

Since I've advised you to look into other author's backgrounds, let me share one more thing... if you are unfamiliar with me, and if this is your first book, I highly recommend you jump to the back and read my bio before you read on. This is not to feed my ego. It is to show you I have been there and done that. I don't write my books from some bullshit perspective—this stuff is my life's work!

At the time of this writing, I'm approaching the midway point of my journey on this planet. So what I'm going to share in the following pages comes from decades of experience. Here is the key point I want you to realize: I never set off after I left the government to be a self-help author or an authority in this field. This profession found me on the long and winding path toward discovering my life purpose. I go into great detail about finding your life purpose in my book *The Simple Life Guide To Decluttering Your Life.* One thing I say in that book is that your life purpose finds you more than you find it. If you told me ten years ago, I would be writing books and changing peoples' lives as a self-help expert, I would have laughed you right out of the room.

Today, I consider it my life's mission to become one of the credible voices in the self-help industry. Yes, in spite of this industry being swarmed with False Prophets, there are some "Torchbearers" who have done a great job in passing on a basic set of self-help principles that have worked for thousands of years. Probably longer. Over the years meeting and talking with these Torchbearers, I have found that we all say the same thing about how we got into this profession...

"I don't need to do this, I have to do this."

In other words, this is more of a calling for us than it is a business. We are just trying to pass down the things we have learned. This is how humans have learned critical life and survival skills for hundreds of thousands of years. If anyone claims that this has changed, or that these principles are out of date because of the advent of technology, they're a moron who doesn't understand basic human nature. I believe that is one of the main reasons so many are struggling today. We no longer are learning from our elders. Instead, we live a "widget in, widget out" lifestyle, hopping from trend to trend, fad to fad learning from the wrong people. Is it any mystery why our lives end up such a shit show after decades of this?

So, I hope this book helps you develop Habits to make you happier, healthier, more prosperous and to live with more purpose and with integrity. If we can accomplish this together, all I ask is that you become a Torchbearer yourself and pass it on. That's what this journey is all about, right? It is not about government bureaucracies, celebrities, or those False Prophets telling us what to do. It is about us taking responsibility for our own actions and for living our own purpose. It's about doing by doing and not waiting for someone else to do it for us. That's why I made integrity the central theme of this book. Living with personal integrity means integrating your Habits with a simple set of principles instead of living by someone else's agenda. This can only happen if you develop and follow the good Habits outlined in this book. I realize this sounds like I'm advising you to live by MY ideas. But as we unpack the principles and Habits in this book, you'll realize that I'm just a torchbearer, and these principles really belong to all of us.

THE FIVE KEY PRINCIPLES FOR LIVING THE SIMPLE LIFE

So, how do you start integrating your Habits with solid principles and start living The Simple Life? Like anything else, you need a set of guiding principles. Otherwise, you're like a pilot without navigational instruments. You're forced to fly by your feelings or to conform to someone else's program. Ask any experienced pilot and they'll tell you that this is a direct path into the cold, cold ground. Likewise, navigating your way to The Simple Life without these principles will eventually land your life on the rocks. You need a solid foundation before you can build a house of success. That's why this is the foundational chapter of the book. These principles will become your compass for living a life of personal Integrity.

Think about the word "integrity" for a moment. Most people think it means doing the right thing. This is somewhat true. But even hard-core criminals can convince themselves they're doing the right thing. The word integrity comes from the word "integration," which means the act of combining many parts in order to form one harmonious whole. People who chase shortcuts are anxious and fleetingly happy because their lives lack this inner harmony. The secret to inner peace and happiness is to integrate your Habits with stable and sound principles. That's what this chapter is about.

I didn't pull these Principles out of thin air. Nor did I repackage them from other self-help books, as a lot of authors do. Rather, I came up with The Five Simple Life Principles almost a decade ago while helping people discover their path to optimal health. These Five Principles are the cornerstone of my philosophy. That's why you'll find them in EVERYTHING I DO.

The Five Simple Life Principles are the result of decades of trial and error. They're the result of my life experience AND my experience working with others. This is why I'm confident that The Simple Life Principles will keep your priorities and deepest values in the FRONT of your mind while you're on your own journey to creating positive and sustainable success through these Fourteen Habits.

As we're exploring these Principles, please resist any impulse to assume that you've *"heard them before."* I realize they might sound similar to things you've already heard. But as we unpack them in detail, I guarantee you'll feel like you're hearing them for the first time. I've also found that even when other self-help authors talk about one of these principles, though sometimes under a different name, they're just repeating things they've heard from other self-help "experts." Many times, they don't really know what they're talking about. Kind of like that Gorilla they taught to type. He could put all the letters of the alphabet together to make words, and he could even string those words into simple sentences. But he was just repeating behavior patterns, without a real understanding of the meaning behind them.

To put this into perspective, imagine having someone tell you about another country, based only on things they've read in a book. This person may think they know what they're talking about. They might even fool a few naïve people with made-up stories about all the things they did while visiting the country. But spending even a day in that other country would quickly show you just how wrong they were. Likewise, I've found that most self-help authors aren't getting to the core of the principles they talk about. They're just filling your head with feel-good dogma that has no practical use in real life. These are the False Prophets I talked about earlier. They keep you trapped on the wrong path by feeding you bad information and selling you products that *seem* to be based on common sense, but that don't produce a lick of real-world results.

So, keep that in mind as we go through these Five Principles and as you start applying them. There's a world of difference between knowing them by memory and *knowing* them by experience.

I've chosen simple names for these principles because it's appropriate for a book on simpler living. I recommend you print them out, and put them somewhere you will see them every day...

1. **Knowledge is Power**
2. **Avoid Extremes**
3. **Keep it Simple**
4. **Something is Better than Nothing**
5. **Take Action Today and Every Day**

As we explore these principles, keep in mind that they deal more with the WHY than the how. We'll get into specific action steps as we talk about the Fourteen Habits. Why have I taken the time to go over *why* to do things and not just *what* to do? Because positive and long-term change is not about fads, quick fixes, or other self-help dogma. Quick, easy fixes are only useful for keeping you Gridlocked.

Principles point the way out because they cut to the "why," which always makes the how much, much more effective.

PRINCIPLE #1: KNOWLEDGE IS POWER

I have a simple philosophy when it comes to anything in life: *Knowledge is Power*. Positive change is far simpler to accomplish and maintain when you're armed with correct, in-depth knowledge.

Dogma Alert: When I say "knowledge," it's important to note that I'm NOT talking about information, which can become an obstacle itself to developing positive and sustainable Habits... I'm not talking about a checklist from an "expert" in personal finance, health or some other subject. We're already swimming in that stuff. If information could make our lives better, fewer people would be frustrated and unfulfilled. I'm talking about knowledge that's been tested and refined by hard-hitting life experiences.

Too many people are trying to undo decades of bad Habits, making bad decisions based on the same bad information, and sleepwalking down the wrong path because they lack the power and guidance of sound, practical knowledge. Almost every day, another article or news program promotes a means to living the "easy life," or "being happy, healthy and more prosperous." Yet, most of this information is just flat-out wrong, often dangerous, and sometimes a bit of both. Most importantly, I've found that people tend to cling to such information, and even defend it, without ever questioning how they came to believe in it.

Haven't you noticed how self-help "knowledge" is often shrouded in vague pseudoscience and cheesy advertising gimmicks? Have you noticed how some politicians and bobble-heads in the media can talk for three to four minutes, using fancy vocabulary to make themselves sound smart, but without really saying anything beyond the obvious? You've probably also heard people talk only from their own experience, or with a rosy-eyed hindsight bias about what made them successful.

They highlight all their smart decisions (which are sometimes no more than dumb luck) and conveniently leave out all the bullshit they had to go through to make their lives better. Is it any wonder why success *appears* so magical to so many people?

Following this kind of advice rarely gets you results. Habits are most effective when you know *why* you're developing them. Otherwise, you're likely to be swayed by the next fad or miracle product that comes along. This happens because you never "owned" your knowledge in the first place. So, keep that in mind while applying this principle in forming your own Habits.

That's why I started with this principle. This book isn't just about information. I'm sharing the knowledge I've gained from decades of trial and error, and from coaching others down this path. Most importantly, the other four principles will help YOU make this knowledge your own.

PRINCIPLE #2: AVOID EXTREMES

Have you noticed how people who read self-help books are chasing a new gimmick every year, or even every month? Ever wonder why they don't stick with one thing long enough to see results? This is because many self-help philosophies deal in unsustainable extremes. They recommend drastic actions that defy the fundamental laws of life. For example, anytime I hear a phrase like *"work just a couple of hours a week and make millions!"* or *"insert product here, in order to cure your blues or feel good about yourself"* I get really pissed off. Why? Because while extreme claims may sound appealing, they don't work in the long run.

Dogma Alert: There's a popular saying that "moderation is the key to happiness." This is not what I mean by "Avoid Extremes." There are things in life that are dumb to even experiment with or to tolerate. There will also be times when making positive change will require you

to get your ass in gear and do things that you believe are "extreme."
But it's important to ask yourself whether you think they're extreme
just because they're counter to the beliefs and the actions that have
kept you stuck. What I'm talking about has more to do with finding
your own natural "rhythm" to living The Simple Life.

Think about how the basic forces of nature create and sustain life. They follow their own natural and effortless rhythm. Night follows day, low tides follow high tides, seasons of scarcity follow seasons of plenty. Many animals that hunt, reproduce, and thrive go into hiding or hibernation for weeks, or months afterward. You might even call these the basic "Habits" of nature. What makes us think we can "skip" these natural rhythms and have everything we want, all the time, in exchange for minimal effort?

If the primordial "Habits" of the natural world follow their own rhythm, why should we assume we can bypass this Principle using some crap shortcut we read on a blog? Once again, people who push shortcuts just want you to buy something you don't need, or to follow some BS philosophy that has no basis in reality. Sure, a slow, steady approach isn't as sexy. It doesn't appeal to your need for instant gratification. I admit that sometimes this even bugs me. But a well thought out plan, followed day after day, week after week, through the repetition of well-paced Habits will deliver positive *sustainable change.* Massive, extreme actions simply can't do that. They'll only burn you out and leave you hunting for the next shortcut!

That said, I confess that, just like everyone else, I have fallen victim to numerous fads and promises of easy living. In fact, I'll tell you about one of my most vivid memories. I was young and trying to improve my health (a goal which makes you a prime target for False Prophets). I remember waking up two or three times a night with a friend to do hundreds of push-ups, sit-ups, pull-ups and other exercises. I remember eating thousands of additional calories my body could never process. It seemed like a good idea at the time. But you might guess what happened. It's the same thing that happens to everyone who follows the "no pain no gain" routines at the other end of the spectrum. You end up fat, exhausted, frustrated, and hungry for the next piece of self-help dogma. Endless stories could be told of fad diets that wreck your metabolism and leave you feeling like you're some freak of nature because "the proven system," didn't work for you.

But these experiences teach us an important lesson: Fads are fads for a reason. They have no grounding in natural principles. They have zero value for the continued pursuit of genuine happiness and accomplishment. The "Fadsters" who push these promises just want to sell you something, anything, that will keep you happy long enough to avoid returning the product for a refund. They don't care whether their product or system works for the long term or not. And when the trick-of-the-month doesn't work, or stops working, guess who's ready to sell you the next miracle product? Pretty soon, you've got a garage full of crap you never use but can't get rid of because you *"might need it someday."*

Finally, let me say that changes made quickly tend to reverse themselves quickly. Extreme measures tend to create extreme backlashes, and sometimes it's impossible to recover from the backlash. But when you follow a plan that respects your own personal rhythms and aligns them with the Habits of the natural world, you enjoy the process more, and the results are much more likely to stick.

PRINCIPLE #3: KEEP IT SIMPLE

The simpler your Habits are, the more energy you can pour into them. Overly complex Habits and strategies, on the other hand, chew up a LOT of your mental energy just trying to keep up with all the details. For example, our culture overcomplicates the pursuit of a healthy happy life by overwhelming us with products, fads, and gimmicks. Again, it's the "widget in, widget out" approach to life. For any result you want, there's a quick-fix widget you can buy. But nature doesn't respect our compulsive need for instant gratification, any more than it allows you to plant a seed, dump gallons of water onto it, and expect the plant to pop up faster because of it. Nature rewards people who integrate their Habits with the laws that govern causes and effects in the real world.

Have you ever run into someone who has found their niche in life? I'm not talking about someone who is complacent and not open to new ideas. I'm talking about that person who is ambitious, responsibly content, relaxed and just flat out enjoying themselves. Everything they do seems to work out effortlessly. And you often wonder why things don't work nearly as well for you. Most people think such people are spending all their waking hours reading blogs, measuring and weighing their food, working out like an Olympic athlete, using every technology-based gizmo promising simplicity. But that couldn't be further from the truth.

People who assume that more-more-more is the secret to happiness and success often end up suffocated under mountains of unnatural and unsustainable Habits.

Successful people, on the other hand, employ simple, well-paced set of Habits for managing their lives. And because their Habits are straight-forward and sustainable, they just keep plugging away at them while everyone else is chasing the next fad or trend. In other words, successful people have a principle-focused approach to life, and they pour most of their mental and physical energy into integrating their Habits with these principles. Not so with most of us. Just think about how much energy and mental bandwidth you've burned up looking for the perfect formula or widget. Take that same amount of time and energy, and pour it into these Fourteen Habits, and you'll be amazed at what you can accomplish in the next three, five, or ten years. Yes, that's longer than the famously promoted thirty, or ninety day success plan. But the advantage is that natural and sustainable Habits work.

Dogma Alert: *Simple does not always equal easy. I bet if you and I sat down, we could list several simple things you can start doing today to dramatically change your life over the next year. Why aren't you already doing these things? Because they're hard. Which I get. In my experience, most of the extreme and overly complicated things we experiment with are merely an attempt to avoid a simple, but difficult set of actions. In fact, marketers often exploit this tendency by selling you products which are supposed to solve the exact problem you're trying to solve. Before you know it, you've got a specialized gadget, book or program for EVERYTHING, but you barely use these things more than once—sometimes not at all.*

That said, it's important to know that the type of simplicity I'm talking about only works for people who have the guts and the motivation to apply it with steadiness and consistency and to avoid extremes.

The saying "less is more" isn't just a clever tagline. It's based on the fundamental law of energy conservation. Again, think about the Habits of the natural world. Birds don't struggle to fly. Fish don't struggle to swim. Trees don't struggle to grow. But it still requires effort. The difference is this energy isn't wasted chasing shortcuts. It's invested into a simple set of sustainable Habits. I hope that by reading my story in chapter two and by following your own path to the simpler life, you will see that this approach is more about subtraction than addition. Just don't assume the subtraction will be easy.

PRINCIPLE #4: SOMETHING IS BETTER THAN NOTHING

At first, overhauling your Habits might seem daunting. Especially if you have deeply engrained Habits or a persistent urge to chase widgets and shortcuts. But here's a thought that always bears repeating:

"Little changes and choices add up."

When it comes to doing nothing versus doing at least something, something is always the right choice. No matter how "small" an action seems. Small actions repeated over time become Habits. And Habits shape our lives. Think of it like dropping a dollar into a piggy bank every hour of the day for years and years… eventually you'd have a nice nest egg. More importantly, you'd develop the *Habit* of saving money, and Habits tend to snowball over time. You'll see as you start applying these Fourteen Habits for yourself.

You can always do something! Instead of bemoaning your stressful and unfulfilling life, answer this question: What would it take to make a better choice in this situation, at this exact moment? Even if it's only an incrementally better option, that little bit counts! Here are a few small tasks you can start with right now…

- Got too much crap in your garage? Make a point to go in there once a week, find something to get rid of, and get rid of it right away. Don't worry about how slow you're going. Just do something.
- Got too much junk food in your diet? Make a point to start cleaning it out of your kitchen. Next time you buy junk food at the grocery store, stop right before you go to the checkout line, and go put at least one junk food item back on the shelf. If you really want to

make a difference, replace it with something from the produce section. Do this with just one item per trip. It will add up.

- Got some debt you want to pay off? Make a point to start paying ten-percent extra on your smallest debt. Not your biggest debt. That's too extreme to start with. Instead, apply Principle #2 and start small. You can tackle your bigger debts once you have some momentum.
- Got too many things running through your mind? Stop and write one of them down in your calendar so you don't have to keep reminding yourself. Don't worry about making a whole list yet. Just start small.

If you read this list, and are thinking *"but, that's not enough,"* you need to read this chapter twice. Anything is enough to start, and if you don't stop, these little actions will become Habits. In time, those Habits will take on a life of their own. After a few days, weeks, or months, you'll start looking for ways to make more positive changes, then a little more, and pretty soon, you won't *want* to stop making positive changes.

Dogma Alert: There's an important difference between patience and complacency, which many of us rarely think about. For example, it's one thing to start by getting rid of one thing in your garage every week. It's an entirely different thing to get rid of one thing a week, only to buy five more things and say "at least I got rid of that _____, something is better than nothing!" This Principle is not meant to inoculate you with overconfidence or to excuse building your life up with one hand while tearing it down with the other. The key is to start with small actions, slowly increasing their frequency and intensity until you find the natural rhythm, we talked about in Principle #2.

Here's one final thing to consider… if you never start because you believe you have to take big actions, you'll stay stuck. So even when circumstances aren't ideal, don't assume you have no control. You can always control something. No matter how small. Instead of feeling bad that you can't do *everything*, do something!

PRINCIPLE #5: TAKE ACTION TODAY AND EVERY DAY

This is the next logical step once you've started taking small actions. Look, America is full of people who *want* to live a better more fulfilling life, but very few ever take action to accomplish this. The difference between the people who dream about it and those who reach their goals is continuous action—and this only comes from forming Habits. Of course, a lot of people have trouble sticking with commitments, but in most cases, it's because they haven't grasped the Four Principles we just covered.

Here's the simplest answer: Happy successful people take action, today and every day. Their lives are an answer to this question:

"What's it going to take to stay on track and make progress today?"

Maybe that means getting up a bit earlier to get to the gym. Maybe it means selling that sports car you really can't afford and buying something more practical. Maybe it means writing that novel you've been talking about for the last ten years. On that point, think about this: ten years is about 3,650 days. A good novel could be 36,500 words or less. Could you write ten words a day? What if you wrote just one-hundred words a day? You would have that novel done in a year! Or, since we're talking about forming positive Habits, maybe it means finding one simple new Habit to reinforce every day.

My point is that small choices add up to a lifestyle that leads to long-term success and happiness. And what are Habits, if not small, repeated choices? Taking big, extreme actions and trying to get the most done in the least amount of time often leads to burnout. Habits, on the other hand, take less and less energy the more engrained they become. That's the real-world truth.

Dogma Alert: There's a difference between the repetition of daily activities and true progress. Unfortunately, it's easy to fool yourself into choosing one over the other. If your actions aren't getting you the results you want, and you've been at them for a while, it's smarter to sit down and rethink your approach instead of just plodding along because you need to check the boxes on your daily to-do list. Thankfully, the other chapters in this book will help you develop Habits and take actions that have already been proven to work.

So, how can you take action today? Every day? Just think back to Principle #4: Something is Better Than Nothing. Maybe you can't get everything done you set out to accomplish today, or this week or this year. But do something. Don't give up and say it is just too hard. Don't get paralyzed by procrastination because things aren't going exactly as you planned. Always ask yourself...

"If I can't do the ideal, what else can I do?" And never start a sentence with *"I can't"* when trying to change your life for the positive, because that is an excuse for *"I won't."* Get in the Habit of saying *"I want to change (X) in my life. Where do I start and how do I do it?"*

I like to call the above "positive change imprinting." I know it sounds really simple. But trust me it works.

Many times, you'll find that the "ideal" is an extreme place to start anyway. Start with something doable and allow yourself to find your own natural rhythm in your own time. For example, what do you do if your car breaks down, and ruins your savings plan for the next couple months? You pick it back up when the repairs are paid for. Then, you put additional money away for unexpected car repairs in the future. Treat this extra savings as part of your repair expenses. Put a little more money away every week. Even ten dollars is better than nothing. Believe me, a day will come when you'll have to pay that money for repairs anyway, so you might as well be ready.

No time for a full workout today? How about taking the stairs instead of the elevator at every opportunity this week? Taking the stairs may be hard the first time. You may not feel like doing it. But a day will come when you'll be glad you ignored that feeling and took action. The most important thing is that you keep things simple and avoid throwing yourself headfirst into a project that's as time-consuming as a part-time job. That might seem smart at first, but it's a recipe for burnout.

Life gets hard. Making better choices is sometimes inconvenient. But you have to ask yourself what kind of future you really want. Want to live debt free or improve your health? The secret is to make the right choices, slowly and surely, today and every day. Today's choices matter. They're under your control. Over time, these choices set the pace for whatever rhythm you get into six months from now, years from now, decades from now. But it all starts with what you do today. This is just as true today as it will be any other day.

That's the hard truth. But the good news is, once these actions become Habits, they'll become easier. And taking consistent action is the secret to integrating your Habits with these principles and finding your rhythm. Again, the more of a Habit your choices become, the less energy it will take for you to repeat those choices every day.

Are you starting to see how these *Five Simple Life Principles* are based on the development of positive and consistent Habits? As I have outlined, short term fixes never work long-term. You must ingrain and practice positive Habits to achieve positive outcomes... it is truly that simple. One thing I can guarantee is that if you do not follow these Five Principles, or if you confuse them with their dogmatic counterfeits, success will be very difficult, if not impossible.

But if you make these Principles a Habitual way of thinking and acting, YOU might be surprised at where you find yourself in another ten years. So, as our first step, let's look at why developing positive Habits is so important for you to be happy and successful in life.

1

WHY GOOD HABITS = A GOOD LIFE

If there is one thing that will define you as a person, it is your Habits. Moreover, if there is one thing which will determine whether you live a life of integrity, it's your Habits. The Habits you acquire and continually work on throughout your life will shape your life and your identity. Simply put, bad Habits lead to a not so good life, but good Habits give you unlimited potential to live the life of your dreams. If you think this sounds too simple, let me be clear that simple does not mean easy. This does take work. Just like anything else worth doing, good Habits are not just one and done. You must continually evaluate and hone your Habits, even after you've formed them. This is the only way to ensure positive and sustainable results. So, I consider Habits the roots of your life from which everything else grows.

What are Habits? They're behaviors you repeat until the behavior is second nature. You know something is a Habit when you no longer have to think about doing it and when you no longer need excessive willpower to stick with it. This is true for good Habits and bad Habits. Of course, we want to focus on the good ones.

Most people think of Habits as these huge behemoths of change. Sometimes they are. But in most cases Habits are just accumulation of small changes, which add up to big changes over time. One or two Habits can make a drastic change for sure. But that doesn't mean you should only have a few good Habits. Habits are continuous—you will always be working on bettering your Habits and adding new ones when necessary. You may also find that some Habits which you thought were good, turn out to be bad for you long term. Smoking is a good example of this. I don't know any teenager who starts smoking because they want to die of a heart attack or of lung cancer in forty to fifty years. They do it to look cool or to destress. But over time, this benefit gets eclipsed by the long-term downfalls of smoking.

HOW DO I FORM POSITIVE HABITS?

Let's revisit The Simple Life Principle #5 *"Take Action Today and Every Day."* Small, daily actions, done consistently, will add up. But, you should also remember Principle #2 *"Avoid Extremes."* Massive actions taken here and there don't add up to much, except burnout. Today we think everything must have and immediate and automatic effect. But that's not the way life truly works. Remember what we said in the last chapter about the "Habits" of nature. It is far harder to make a massive change in a very short time. That is where most people fail to make positive change—when they don't get the result they want immediately, they throw in the towel. Don't be that person! This is the kind of person who has no sense of their authentic self because they're always chasing new widgets, or systems, in search of a "shortcut."

In my other books, I talk about how to escape the daily anxiety and monotony of living in what I call "The Grid." The Grid is a network of society-wide beliefs, systems and institutions which are designed to turn us into commodities. This is why so many people don't live with real integrity. They're too busy conforming. You'll see what I'm talking about as you read this book. For example, just think about how many industries and institutions profit from promising you pleasure today at the expense of tomorrow's dreams. Nothing sells like good old gain without pain and instant gratification, right? In my experience, most of the "experts" in our society are the architects of the beliefs, systems and institutions, which make us slaves to The Grid and its lifestyle. These Gridmasters count on you and me to learn, and to repeat Habits that will move money out of your pocket into theirs and help them maintain their positions of power and privilege. The only way out of this Gridlocked Lifestyle is to replace those beliefs and Habits with ones that will empower you.

THE SELF-FULFILLING PROPHECY OF FAILED NEW YEAR'S RESOLUTIONS

As I write this, it is the beginning of another new year, when historically people try to make changes in their health. You know, the good old New Year's Resolution! Why someone would wait until a new year to make change in their life baffles me. Changing your life for the positive is a constant life-long endeavor. If you assume this is more likely to happen because you align your decision to change your life with the calendar, you're setting yourself up for failure. First of all, waiting for a certain time of the year to do something positive is no way to form Habits. You form Habits from what you do consistently, rain or shine. Just think about how silly it is to try and learn positive Habits by saying...

"I'll do that at the beginning of the year as one of my New Year's Resolutions."
Or...

"I'll start working on this goal once the kids are back in school."
Or...
"I'll start my diet after the Holidays are over."
Or...
"I'll start my business after this financial slump has passed and the stock market is up again."

This is a piss poor way to change your life. It doesn't help you build personal integrity because you're hinging your success on exterior circumstances instead of on your own resourcefulness and determination. In fact, we should start calling them "New Year's Procrastinations for Failure" instead of "New Year's Resolutions." After all, how resolute are you if you don't start working on your positive Habits the second you get the idea? The sooner you start a positive Habit, the more time you have to benefit from that Habit and the more you benefit from the initial momentum of acting right away instead of putting things off.

You have to look at positive Habits as an investment that compounds over time, just like your 401k retirement account. The more positive Habits you have, and the more energy you put into them, the more potential they will have to pay off in the future. Also, the more positive Habits you have, the less likely negative Habits will find their way into your life and the more inner peace and happiness you'll have.

HOW TO MAKE THE MOST OF THIS BOOK

I didn't pick Fourteen Habits just because I like the number. In fact, I started out with just Twelve Habits, and added the Thirteenth and Fourteenth Habits because I've found them to be essential to living with integrity. As we go through these Habits, I will give you the action for making these positive Habits part of your routine. These Habits will become automatic behavior patterns. Most importantly, these action steps will help you crystalize these Habits into belief. This is the secret to escaping the grip of the Gridmasters. As we unpack these action steps, just remember Principle #4 *"Something is Better Than Nothing."* If you do nothing, nothing changes. If you do a little bit every day, a lot will change over time. You just have to ditch the instant gratification mindset and start thinking about momentum and growth.

More importantly, start thinking of all the things you want to change in your life. What Habits can you implement in order to accomplish these? Write them down... that is a positive Habit within itself. If you can't think of any Habits, don't worry. That's why I wrote this book, and these Habits are universal and timeless enough to work for anyone and for accomplishing almost any goal.

One thing I can guarantee is that if you continue to follow the "instant gratification" mindset of the Grid, your actions will not become Habits. Habits need time to incubate and to find their way into your permanent beliefs and behavior patterns. There is no magic formula. Everyone's relationship with these Habits is highly personal, and so is the time frame for these Habits to pay off. So, never give up on your positive Habits, because they seem to not be working right now or because they're working much quicker for someone else than they are for you. That person might just be better at getting started, while you might be better at sticking with your Habits long term. And I'll take the long-term advantage any day over a quick start. Long-term success leads to real peace and happiness because you come to a place where you no longer have to over-think shit or use excessive willpower to "stick to your commitments." Instead, you just live your authentic life and enjoy every day of it.

Let me give you a perfect example from my life about sticking with a Habit and being rewarded later down the road. I started my journey to becoming a writer in 2010 I had no back-ground as a writer. Well, except writing criminal investigative reports, and trust me that is not even close to the same. Matter of fact, I sucked at English and writing throughout most of my life. I was a math guy. But I also have a very creative side and love teaching. So, when I first started my pursuit of a possible writing career, I was not very good. Not at all. But I kept at it, and developed Habits overtime, which made me better and better. One of the most valuable Habits I have acquired over the years is using a well thought out outline to make sure my writing has solid organization. From the beginning of my writing career, I have been creating this outline before I even write one word of the manuscript, and I still do this today. This Habit saves me a ton of time, and more importantly makes my editors job a lot easier. It also makes my books much more readable and memorable.

By creating and sticking to this Habit, I now make a full-time living as a writer. Yes, it took ten years. But if I hadn't stuck with that Habit, it would have been much harder for me to get to this point. Hell, there is a good chance I may not have made it at all. Obviously, there are many other Habits I have developed over my writing career. But starting very book with a well thought out outline is one of the most important.

Here is another timely example. As a recent Harvard Study estimates, half the population of America will be considered obese by 2030. As I have discussed in many of my writings, health is an area that we struggle in this country at an alarming rate. Why? I feel it is because people want immediate results and refuse to understand or to accept that optimal health is a life-long journey. It's a journey that requires hard work and good Habits for the rest of your life! I know this firsthand because I have worked with a lot of clients over the years who wanted me to "fix them" in two weeks, after they'd spent their entire life destroying their health. Of course, the Gridmasters and False

Prophets have no problem telling you this because they KNOW you'll buy their product if they tell you want you want to hear. But the truth is, it takes a bare minimum of eating healthy for thirty days before you even start seeing results. For you to see real *long-term* results you need to stick with a health program for a year. And then guess what? You need to continue and improve what you are doing for the remainder of your life to maintain those results. That is how Habits influence your long-term health!

That's where this saying comes from...

"I'm an overnight success that only took ten years to accomplish."

The belief in overnight success is one of the Sacred Dogmas of The Grid. In real life, results only come as the result of your consistent Habits. Can you show me someone who is over-weight and unhealthy as a result of consistently eating healthy and exercising? Can you show me someone who is broke as a result of living within their means and saving their extra money? Of course you can't, because that person doesn't exist. Oh trust me, I have had many clients who have come to me and say...

"I don't understand why I'm overweight and don't feel good... I do everything right!"

But when I dig into their eating and exercise routines, I almost always find a long list of **BAD** Habits.

That said, I think this is a perfect time to transition into the first Habit and talk about the one thing that stops most people from ever developing positive Habits...

STEVEN PRESSFIELD - THE WAR OF ART

"Most of us have two lives. The life we live, and the unlived life within us. Between the two stands Resistance."

2

HABIT 1 - STOP WHINING AND BLAMING OTHERS

L et's go right to the heart of the matter why most of us never reach our true potential. We have become so soft in our easy access-to-everything society. In most cases, more than we truly deserve. We think we are ENTITLED to a happy joyful life of abundance. When we don't get what we want, we throw a tantrum and blame everyone else around us. We instantly jump to the "I'm the victim of circumstances out of my control" mentality. We say childish and ridiculous things like...

"Those evil ____ are keeping me down."
"I grew up poor."
"I'm not smart."
"I have all these health problems."
"I don't have enough money, or enough time."
"I have kids."
"My parents didn't give me enough attention."
"My cat thinks I'm a loser."

...on and on and on.

THE SIMPLE LIFE GUIDE TO SMALL HABITS FOR BIG CHANGE

Here is a point I want to drive home right away…

"No matter how hard your life is, or what you have gone through, someone has it much harder, and has struggled a great deal more in life than you."

There's a good reason I use this in all my speaking engagements. To this day I have never met the person who is ranked #1 on "hardest life list." So stop thinking it is you, because it is not. Especially if you live in the good old United States of America. We are the most prosperous country on the planet, and everyone has the potential to live the life of their dreams. The only person standing in your way is YOU! Not your boss. Not your kids. Not your spouse. Not your politicians. You! Living with integrity starts with accepting that your life is your responsibility, not someone else's. People who don't get this end up surrendering their power to the people they blame.

Do you know where this "I'm a victim" attitude comes from? It comes from us allowing ourselves and others to become perpetual whiners. And today, if you call someone out for their whining you are instantly labeled as "shaming" them. As a result, all of us are allowed to screw up our lives as much as we want, without being called out for our mistakes. All because people are afraid of offending someone. As a result, we're all digging a hole into ideocracy and failure. We dig our own graves while everyone stands aside and watches, too afraid to ask us what the hell we're doing or why we're doing it. Personally, I would rather have someone smack me in the face and take the shovel out of my hands.

Trust me, I have calluses from digging some pretty deep holes of stupidity in my life. I was a "Class A Whiner" after I left the government. It took me some time to realize that I was the main cause of my unhappiness. I had lost my path in life. I took a couple left hand turns when I should have taken a right, and I was off the road and half in the ditch because of it. I wasted time crying about how things were just so unfair. I complained that people just didn't understand my situation, which was complete bullshit. I bet most of us would be shocked to learn how many other people are telling themselves the same thing... that their life is harder than everyone else's, and no one could possibly understand how hard.

THE FREE GIFT THAT TOO MANY PEOPLE WASTE

This is a good time to talk about the concept of "Free Will." Free Will is a philosophy that says we decide our fate, we make our own decisions. Simply put, the philosophy of Free Will tells us that we are in control of our lives. I know there are many factors that can determine the outcome of our life. But by choosing Free Will, you put yourself in the driver's seat. Free Will is how you respond to circumstances, no matter what they may be. This is what determines your direction and lot in life.

Here is a passage from the song "Freewill" by the famous progressive rock band Rush—I think this will drive the concept of Free Will home:

You can choose a ready guide
In some celestial voice
If you choose not to decide
You still have made a choice
You can choose from phantom fears
And kindness that can kill
I will choose a path that's clear
I will choose free will.

Some are probably thinking...

"What the heck does this have to do with positive Habits and me taking responsibility for my actions?"

Let me explain a bit further by focusing on this line...

"If you choose not to decide—You still have made a choice."

In other words, if you decide to do nothing, you are still exercising your power of Free Will. So why not use your Free Will to make a choice for the better? I consider whining about things instead of doing something about them to be a choice of inaction... you're literally choosing not to decide. To make it worse, I consider whining a form of negative inaction—a double whammy of freely and willingly screwing up your life!

The bottom line is, it is much easier to complain and whine about why you can't do something than it is to pull up your big boy pants and just get it done. Now, there are some logical reasons for taking the easy way out when it presents itself. Humans, just like any organism on this planet, use energy conservation as a survive and thrive technique. Imagine being a hunter-gather and having to chase the fastest, smartest, and sometimes the most dangerous animals for food. Imagine trying to do this with no thought behind your actions. Imagine blaming the Wooly Mammoth for being too strong to take down, or blaming the gazelle for being too fast, or blaming your competitors (animal and human) for hoarding food and refusing to share with you. You would be expending a great deal of mental and emotional energy without replacing those calorie stores. You'd be all output with no input. You would literally starve to death, simply because you weren't thinking or paying attention to your actions and their consequences. If you had a family, they would die too. Most important, you'd die because you were too busy whining and complaining to do something about your own survival.

HOW THE "EASY WAY" JUST MAKES LIFE HARDER

You must realize that while the easy way is almost always the most desirable way, that doesn't mean it is the best way. Taking shortcuts today is a pretty good indicator that you'll end up paying for it tomorrow. You have to overcome your genetic tendency to conserve energy in order to be successful. We are no longer in a daily battle of life and death. If our genetics "knew" this, they would immediately rewire themselves to avoid the easy road. But our bodies don't know this, and that's what we're up against. The good news is, we can defy this natural tendency by forming positive and sustainable Habits. But that starts with dropping the "my problems are someone else's fault" mentality.

I know this may seem to an odd explanation to some. After all, we haven't had to live as hunter-gathers for thousands of years now. But once you realize you are wired to take the easy way, you'll have the self-awareness to overcome it by forming positive Habits. Remember Principle #1 "Knowledge is Power." And the most important piece of knowledge you'll gain in the beginning, is how YOU are screwing up your own life, and that you are responsible for changing it. That's why we started with this Habit.

People have a horrible Habit of just wanting the HOW and not the WHY. We want to know how to fix our problems. But without the why, the how is just something you follow blindly without understanding the reason(s) you are doing it. This is how you become a mindless victim of The Grid, instead of a self-empowered agent of Free Will. This is also why most people don't live with real integrity. People who live by principles (instead of by shortcuts) don't have to blame others for their own mistakes and misfortunes. They take responsibility for living a life true to themselves, and that's the source of their happiness.

INTEGRATING HABIT #1

Let's dig into the beliefs and the action steps for this first Habit so we can stop whining and blaming others…

1. Things go wrong… deal with it and move on.
2. Don't worry about things that you can't change and/or that are in the past.
3. Life is hard. That is just a fact. Stop thinking you are the only person affected by this, because you're not.
4. Every problem has a solution. It just depends how much effort you are willing to put into the solution.
5. Start listening to yourself when you make excuses. Write your rationalizations down and figure out a way to counteract them. Remember that piece of advice I gave you in the Five Principles… never start a sentence with "I can't" start it with "I want to do (X). What do I need to learn and implement to accomplish this?"
6. Stop comparing yourself to others. This means comparing yourself to people who are better and better off, or to people who are worse or worse off. Everyone takes their own path and has their own goals in life.
7. Failure may not be an option, but one thing is certain, at some point you will fail. In some cases, spectacularly. But it is not your failures that define you as a person. It's how you react to those failures that matters.
8. Blaming others for your problems accomplishes absolutely nothing. Sure, you may have some bad luck from time to time, but so does everyone else. Redirect that negative energy into positive action.
9. Stay away from people who reinforce your tendency

to blame others. In other words, that "friend" who makes excuses on your behalf isn't helping you. They're just teaching you how to be a victim. Find people who will be honest about your mistakes.

10. Stop demanding that other people "fix" what they've broken in your life. Even if they were ninety-nine-percent in the wrong when they hurt you. The odds of them fixing their own mistakes is very slim and expecting them to do so will just make you angry, bitter and unhappy.

3

HABIT 2 - DON'T BE AN ASSHOLE

M ost people will probably read this and say…

"But I'm not an asshole."

Unfortunately, I have found today that this is rarely the case. With advent of the "look at me" movement, which I feel social media is hugely responsible for, we have completely forgotten just how easy it is to be dickish. We like to hide our newfound narcissism by preaching togetherness and other virtues because it makes us feel better, while acting completely the opposite. So, when I say "don't be an asshole," it's important to understand that I'm NOT talking about whether you consider yourself an asshole. It's easy to lie to yourself and others about that. I'm talking about what your behaviors say about you.

It's hard to keep this in check when you lack basic human interaction. And by that, I mean actually communicating with someone face to face instead of through a computer or smart-phone. As I have explained in some of my previous books, humans have historically survived (it appears for possibly millions of years) by building small social groups. These groups usually had less than 50, up to 150 people, and these numbers are significant. They're in the range of what's known as Dunbar's Number.

Dunbar's Number is based on a theory that the human brain expanded rapidly at one point, in order to have the bandwidth to convey our emotions, thoughts and desires. Even early humans had an incredibly complex communication system, and so our brains had to expand to accommodate this. Simply put, the theory states that our complex way of communication is our main survival mechanism.

And when I say "communication," I'm not just talking about language. We have five primary senses: touch, smell, taste, hearing and sight. These are critical survival senses and are used in many ways. One important function of these senses is deciphering whether someone is friend or foe. But communicating through proxy, as you do by using social media, only allows you to use two of those senses (hearing and sight) in a very limited manner, when compared to a person-to-person setting.

Not to mention, there's a very good scientific reason people are more likely to act dishonest, or like assholes, when they're not communicating face to face. The human brain is fit with a network of neurons called "mirror neurons." These neurons cause you to, at some level, feel an emotional connection to another person's suffering or pleasure. It's as if your mirror neurons are reflecting the other person's experience inside your mind. This is why it's harder to be cruel to someone in person. Your mirror neurons pick up the hurt in their eyes or on their face, and you literally feel a connection to their pain. But not on social media. There, you can call someone all kinds of horrible names, and not feel a thing. In fact, a great test of whether you're a dick is to ask yourself if you're meaner to strangers on social media than you are face to face.

I feel that social media has created millions of new assholes, (not to mention the assholes who create these platforms) therefore I consider it to be the most destructive human interaction mechanism ever created. People who follow me already know that this is why I'm not a big fan of social media. Here's a perfect example of what I'm talking about...

A not-so-tough guy loves trolling social media, creating all kinds of drama by telling random people they're stupid, or idiots, for not believing what he believes. First of all, he doesn't know these people and they don't know him. So his thoughts and the other person's thoughts are going through a virtual-reality-like filter that the human brain has a hard time comprehending. Because of this, social media has brought about an entirely new level of behavior in which someone acts in an aggressive manner who would not usually act this way in person. Basically, social media allows a self-proclaimed "tough" guy to act like an asshole without any real-life repercussions, such as being punched in the mouth. People can also create fake accounts with aliases and play make-believe as much as they want when they are using social media. It's much more difficult to hide behind an alternative personality when you're interacting face to face. In fact, if you spend more time interacting with people on social media than you do in real life, my guess is your "offline life" is more stressful and chaotic than it needs to be. This, again, is because the less time you spend being who you really are, the harder you have to work to keep up the façade. If you want peace, you need principles and Habits to simplify and ground your real-life behaviors.

All of that said, do you act as I have outlined above while on social media? I hope not, but if you do, you need to have some deep introspection about who you are as a person.

YOU MIGHT BE AN ASSHOLE IF...

Since it's so easy to lie to ourselves about this Habit, here's a list of behaviors that will tell you whether you're acting like an asshole...

1. You insult people on forums and social media sites, even if you've never met them in person.
2. You talk trash about people when they're not around instead of working out your problems with them.
3. You have people in your life who you only call when you need something from them.
4. When you get home from work, you start complaining to your spouse or kids (or asking them for things) before you greet them and ask how their day was.
5. You think anyone who votes for or represents the "other" political party is a bad person, and often tell them so.
6. When someone else is talking, you often find yourself thinking about what you want to say next.
7. You often interrupt people mid-sentence because you think you know what they're going to say.
8. You "cancel" appointments with people by simply not showing up. When they call to ask why, you don't pick up the phone or even text them.
9. You break off relationships by text, or by social media, instead of meeting the person face to face or even over the phone.
10. You litter because you're too lazy to look for a trash can.
11. You leave a lousy tip for your server, not because they gave horrible service, but because the restaurant they

work for screwed something up or took too long to deliver your food.

12. You don't flush the toilet when you're using a public restroom.

13. You text or surf the web on your smartphone while you're out at dinner (or just talking) with your friends or family.

14. You argue with the checkout person at a store over something trivial while people are waiting in line behind you.

15. When you're talking on the phone in public, you talk so loud everyone around you can hear your conversation.

16. You report people on social media when they post something you find "wrong" or offensive.

17. You don't wait your turn at a four way stop.

18. You spam people via instant message on Facebook or LinkedIn.

19. Post photos on social media, and tag people who aren't even in them, just to get your picture seen by more people.

20. You often butt into other people's conversations without permission.

21. You're overweight, but you only buy one seat on the airplane and force the people next to you to live with the consequences of your poor eating decisions.

I could list more, but are you starting to notice a pattern? All of these scenarios lack the key ingredient of being a decent person...

EMPATHY – THE CURE FOR DICKHEADEDNESS

Virtual communication toys (like social media), have greatly altered and distorted our ability to feel empathy for others. Empathizing with another person means you can put yourself in their shoes and *feel* what they feel. When you say something hateful or are being a jerk in person, you will get a reaction, good or bad from the people around you. You'll get physical queues from them, like body-language, voice tone, and facial expressions (emoticons don't count). You'll also experience chemical releases in response to other people, such as sweat, reddening of the face, tears, or maybe even a smack upside your head. These will change the way you interact with people. Social media basically short circuits this communication process and gives you only a one-dimensional view of the other person. Of course, this is not just about social media, as we have been driven towards a "me" society today in general.

Have you noticed how most people are only concerned about themselves, everyone else be damned? If you haven't noticed this, maybe you were born after the year 2000 and you've come to think of this selfishness epidemic as normal. I get that. But ask someone who remembers a world before the internet and smartphones. Ask them about how people treated each other then, compared to how they do now. Trust me, they are NOT exaggerating. The irony is that people who talk a big game about how people should act, normally act totally the opposite of what they preach. Don't be one of those people. Don't just dismiss this chapter and tell yourself that you're different. Really take an honest look at the checklist in this chapter. Or, better yet, have someone you trust go over it with you and ask them to be honest with you. Preferably someone who remembers life before social media and smartphones. I bet you'll learn a lot about yourself.

As I said above, communication is the most important skill

us hairless apes have. From the little bit we know about ourselves, our ability to communicate at a high level, is what separates us from all other animals. Someday we may learn that our dog has an ability to communicate at a very high level, but for now, let's go with what we know.

In their paper "Natural Language and Natural Selection," researchers Steven Pinker and Paul Bloom theorize that a series of calls or gestures evolved over time into combinations, giving us complex communication, or language. As humans learned more about how to best survive, they developed a need to communicate these survival methods to others in their tribe.

Simply put, if you want to avoid being a raging asshole, you must learn how to communicate and to understand what others are trying to communicate to you. Again, don't assume you've got this figured out until you've taken an honest look at yourself. Living with integrity starts with accepting that your life is your responsibility, not someone else's. And this starts with accepting the good and bad parts of yourself.

For example, listening has become a lost art, and if you want to pretty much guarantee people will see you as an asshole—be a terrible listener. People are not born being good listeners. It is a skill that must be learned and improved with time. If you cannot listen, you will never be good at empathizing and relating to what others are feeling. We all have our opinions and we all want to be heard. That's normal. But one of the most critical skills you can have is the ability to shut up and pay attention to what someone is trying to tell you. Sometimes it may be something you don't want to hear, but that is life… get over it!

I know this firsthand. As some of you may know, I can be pretty opinionated. The one thing I have changed drastically over the last decade, besides my health, which we'll talk about later, is my ability to be a good listener. If you want to have positive and formative interactions with people, this is something you are going to have to develop. And remember, language isn't the only kind of communication. There's also body language, facial expressions, and tones of voice. Being a good "listener" means being able to discern those as well.

People are amazed that I refuse to do business with someone who is not referred to me by a friend or that I have not met one on one. Now I have a lot of experience conducting interviews, and interrogations, but I will tell you the best way to figure out what someone is all about is through face to face interaction. If you want to take things to the next level, you must be able to empathize with that person. It's how real trust is developed.

To emphasize this point, I'll close this chapter with a perfect example from my past as a criminal investigator. Back then, I was known as the guy who could pretty much get a confession out of anybody. No, not by beating them over the head with a phone book. I could do it just by talking to them and understanding how they got into the situation they were in. For instance, I would always have the potential target of my investigation meet me somewhere public, like a fast food restaurant or coffee shop—not an interrogation room. This would put them at ease and make them more apt to opening up. I did this because I had noticed people act very differently when I would question them in my office. I also always started my interviews with basic conversation such as...

"Are you married, have any kids, what are some of your favorite things to do?"

Just basic chit-chat. It wasn't an act or me trying to trick them, it is just how I am. I like learning about people, and the fact that they were a possible target or witness to a criminal investigation didn't change that.

By learning about them first, I'd build trust before asking

more pointed questions about their possible criminal activity. I found that the more they felt they could trust me, the more information they would share. I also learned that, in most cases, many of them were just like you and me. They had just made some bad decisions in life. Of course, these were white collar criminals, (mostly financial crimes). So we're not talking about violent offenders. But this tactic has even been known to work in murder cases. It works because at our core, we're all human beings who just want to be heard. Which is why I suggest becoming a good listener. You'll be shocked at what people will want to tell you if you just shut up and listen instead of waiting for your turn to talk.

INTEGRATING HABIT #2

1. Listen, listen and listen! Being a good listener is the key to being a better person. It goes hand in hand with Principle #1 "Knowledge is Power." If you want to be informed and to gain knowledge, you need to be a good listener. I have never learned anything by listening to my own voice. Well, besides how stupid I am sometimes.

2. Ask people close to you what you can do to be a better person. Are there things you can improve that they may find assholish? You will be surprised what you will get back when you actually ask an honest straight-forward question like this. When you get your answers, make a list of the top five things to change and start working on them.

3. Start watching peoples' body language when you are having a conversation—an estimated sixty-percent of human communication is done through body language. Watch for facial expressions and listen to

the tone of their voice. Don't try to decode any of this either. Just pay attention until you start developing an intuitive instinct for what people are thinking and feeling.

4. Meditate on a regular basis. I have been meditating for almost a decade now, and I can tell you firsthand —I'm a better person for it. It teaches you to be patient and to quiet your own mind. Which obviously makes it easier to pay attention to others.

5. Make your health a priority. The better you feel the more understanding and nicer you tend to be. This might seem out of place, but I'll explain why in the next chapter.

6. Pay attention to how you treat people when they're at work serving you. For instance, start a conversation with the person who picks up your trash, your server at a restaurant, the person who rings up your groceries, or answers your customer service calls. You can tell a lot about someone by how they treat people who can't help them or hurt them.

7. Give people a chance to overcome your first impression of them. Unless you're in a profession that requires you to get a quick read on people, your first impressions of people probably aren't as accurate as you think they are. Try reserving judgement about people until you've spent some time getting to know them.

8. Do things for people just for the sake of doing them. In other words, do something to help someone in need, and don't tweet or post about it on Facebook to try and impress the world with how good you are. Advertising your virtues is a pretty good sign that you're only helping people to make yourself look

good. Pick a way to do things for others, and let as few people know about it as possible.

9. Stop trying to "outdo" other people. Some competition is healthy. But too much is destructive for your emotional state and for your relationships. If you're going to try and be better than someone, try being better than the person you were yesterday.

10. Next time you're debating someone you disagree with, make it your number one priority to understand their position first. Even better, see if you can get them to confirm that you've understood their position. Too often, we don't do this because we're afraid that understanding someone's point means we're somehow agreeing with it. You can overcome this fear (and avoid a lot of fights) by trying to understand someone before launching a counterargument.

4

HABIT 3 - TREAT YOUR BODY LIKE A TEMPLE

Some of you who have followed me for years may be wondering why this Habit wasn't the first on our list. In most of my books, I pound the importance of your health from the get-go. This is because I consider focusing on your health such an important Habit that I made it the first leg of my "Three-Legged Stool" which is the cornerstone of The Simple Life Philosophy. By the way, I cover the Three-Legged Stool of The Simple Life in detail in my short book: *The Simple Life – Life Balance Reboot.*

So why not make it the first Habit? First off, because you can be healthy and still be a whiner and an asshole. It's also true that people in poor health often blame other people for something they should be taking responsibility for. Habit #1 is the way to get out of that trap and start taking action. So, I thought it would make more sense to cover those two Habits first.

Readers who are not familiar with my writings and The Simple Life Philosophy, are probably scratching their heads right now thinking, *"What does my health have to do with making me more successful in life?"* I'll say with 100 percent confidence: everything! I've been involved in the areas of health and athletics for over four decades, and I've learned that our declining health is the biggest factor (just behind life purpose) in our overall lack of drive, life satisfaction, and happiness. Truly living The Simple Life starts with sustainable health Habits. If you don't make this your number one priority in the pursuit of simple living, everything else I cover in *this book* will be far, far more difficult to implement.

If you doubt this, just ask yourself how many times one of the following excuses has stopped you from doing something...

"I don't have enough energy."
"I'm too tired to do it now."
"I'm too tired to think about this."
"I don't feel good today."

In fact, read my "you might be an asshole if..." list from the last chapter, and ask yourself how often you do those things simply because you're too tired to make a better choice. I think this is why Vince Lombardi said "Fatigue makes cowards of us all." Cowards lack the strength to live by their own principles. I'd simply add that chronic self-induced fatigue also makes assholes of us all.

Your energy level is directly related to your overall health, mental, physical, and emotional. That's why developing positive and sustainable health Habits is so important. Now, this section will not be an all-inclusive guide on how to get healthy. Instead, we'll focus on starting to implement some basic health Habits. If you really want to get ambitious about this, my book *The Simple Life Guide To Optimal Health: How to Get Healthy and Feel Better Than Ever* is an A to Z guide to nutrition, basic exercise and supplementation.

Let me start by saying that if you expected me to solve all your health problems in one chapter of this book, go back to

Habit #1 and read it again. Trust me, I have met a lot of people in my life who expect me to fix decades of health issues and get them on track in a one-hour consultation or by emailing them "the how-to's" (for free I may add). You have got to be kidding me… right? As with anything, getting your health on track takes hard-work and dedication, especially in the beginning. If anyone promises you some magic formula, such as drink a glass of water when you first wake-up, as a key to their health and self-help philosophy, that person is a False Prophet and should be treated like one. I have decades of experience in the health world, and I KNOW that these idiots have very little or no knowledge in health. They are just placating you by selling you "the easy way" of doing things. Let the self-help tourists waste their time reading those books. We've got real work to do.

GETTING HEALTHY STARTS WITH PRINCIPLE #1: KNOWLEDGE IS POWER

In my book *Life Balance Reboot,* I make it 100 percent clear that you can't get healthy unless you know and accept just how unhealthy you really are. Remember Principle *#1: Knowledge is Power.* And when it comes to your health, self-knowledge is just as important as knowing what to eat, what not to eat, and what kind of exercises to do. It might even be more important. It's how you gain the motivation to get your butt in gear.

Over the last decade, I've helped a lot of people find their path to optimal health. When it comes to developing positive long-lasting Habits, health has to be the one people struggle with the most. But here is the key I want to drive home. Once you establish your health Habits by creating a system you can follow, you will wonder why you struggled so mightily in the past. People are shocked that even though my health is the most important aspect of my life (it should be yours as well), I spend very little time on it, when compared to most people who are unhealthy today.

The primary reason, I have spent decades establishing positive Habits—once it becomes a Habit you don't even realize it is something you are doing on a consistent basis—it becomes second nature.

I do want to get into the nitty-gritty of our health epidemic in this country though, as it seems to be getting much worse.

During the last five years I've noticed Americans are growing (rounder, not taller) at an alarming rate. After talking to some other individuals in the realm of health, I asked them if they were witnessing the same thing as I was, and to my surprise all said yes. This tells me most people need to rethink what they mean by being "in shape."

After finding this out, I decided to run a little experiment. For the last year, no matter where I've been, I've stopped for a bit to observe the people around me to see how long it would take to find an obese person. I had no prerequisites (age, gender, race, etc.), other than whether the person appeared to be obese.

Let's be clear on what I mean by obese, because it's easy to fool yourself on this point. Today, obesity is determined by our Body Mass Index (BMI). BMI is calculated by taking a person's weight in kilograms and dividing it by the square of their height in meters. But BMI does not measure body fat directly. Meaning, a bodybuilder with shoulders the size of dinner plates and four-percent body fat would still be considered "obese."

So obviously, I didn't use this formula in my experiment, as I couldn't ask the person I observed to come over and let me measure them to determine their BMI. But with my experience in health, I've got a pretty good idea of what people should weigh in relation to their height. I simply considered someone obese if they appeared to be fifty or more pounds overweight. Of course, this is not a highly scientific study. But I'm using it to show you just how much our health is in decline today.

When I first started this experiment, I knew it would be easy to find obese people, but what I found was truly shocking. On average, it took me less than thirty seconds to find one. Sometimes it took less than ten seconds to find someone who was most likely obese by today's medical standards. What I really didn't expect is that in most cases I found them to be what I would consider dangerously obese (100 pounds or more overweight).

What saddened me more were the people I would consider able-bodied, but who were severely overweight and rolling around in electric scooters. Other than their weight, they appeared to have no physical disability that would cause them to need a scooter. Matter of fact, I witnessed several people get up out of their scooter and walk to their car once they were done shopping.

Folks, we don't just have an obesity problem. We have a full-blown public health epidemic on our hands!

If you think this sounds mean or uncompassionate consider how you'd feel if we were pointing out the amount of people who had another life-threatening condition, like cancer. What if the objective was to draw attention to this devastating disease so people could make better choices and avoid dying young because of it? Well, the National Institutes of Health tell us that obesity (and being overweight) are the second most common cause of *preventable* death in the United States. Tobacco related illnesses were the first. We have marches for cancer, diabetes, and dozens of other deadly diseases. Yet, we ignore the dangers of obesity? Hell, if anyone needs to do a little extra walking, it's them. Yet, we're supposed to stay silent about this because WE don't want to appear insensitive? I say that's not very compassionate.

Besides, if you think I'm "fat shaming" or being mean, this book is not for you anyway. If you have a problem with an honest observation about a life-threatening condition as a means of creating urgency about solving it, I think that's sad. And if you're someone who criticizes people like me as "fat shamers," maybe you ought to ask yourself whether you're only doing that to make yourself appear more noble or compassionate.

This book was written to help people who are looking to make positive changes in their lives. And in order to make changes, you need to identify the problem(s) and solve them— plain and simple. Positive change can be painful, and most lessons in life are learned from things that don't come easy. Getting better takes honesty, hard work, and not giving up.

Since we're talking about outward appearances, I'll add that your health is not only about feeling better and looking good in a bathing suit. While editing this book, I had a friend who lost a thirty-five year-old-family member to a massive heart attack. And he was at an ideal weight and would have passed an obesity test. That said, I believe it affects almost everything in your life, including:

- Energy Level
- Sex Drive
- Memory
- Willpower
- Stamina
- Stress Level
- Confidence
- Sleep Cycles

People who overeat are also impulsive about eating out and shopping at the grocery store, which hurts their financial life. So, why do so many out of shape people THINK they're in shape? Probably because they've been out of shape so long, they forgot how good their energy level, sex drive, memory and willpower used to be, or they never had it to begin with.

I hope you can now see why your health is so important. It's the one thing that you can change right here, right now. And once you get control of your health, you've taken a huge step in controlling everything else in your life. You're also that much closer to living a life true to yourself and your principles.

COMBINING THIS HABIT WITH HABIT #1 AND PRINCIPLE #1

Now that I've offended some of you (maybe more than once at this point), let me clarify something. If I had a nickel for every person I've consulted with on their health that has told me *"I have a bad metabolism, I'm big boned, I'm disabled etc.,"* I would be a very rich man. When it comes to excuses, health has to be ranked number-one in the *"it's not my fault"* category. In fact, I have a friend who has written advertising copy for nearly twenty years, and he tells me that the phrase *"it's not your fault,"* is one of the most common (and effective) phrases for the marketing of diet products.

We've become so soft and gooey in today's society that we pretty much have an excuse for everything (again that is where Habit #1 comes in). I know, as I've used them myself. We now call obesity and being overweight a disease. But I can't say it any plainer than this: Making poor life choices in the area of health is not a disease! How we've decided that eating poorly and not getting enough exercise is somehow a disease is appalling to me. Yet, society has given us a built-in excuse to waddle through life —don't address the problem, just buy a pair of stretchy pants and blame everyone else!

Disease is defined as: an illness of people, animals, plants, etc., caused by infection or a failure of health rather than by an accident. I like how the motivational speaker Zig Ziglar said it: that he used to be thirty-pounds overweight, and that he was overweight by choice, because he had *"never eaten anything on accident."* I'm pretty sure donuts don't fall into our mouths by accident. And our butts don't become the size of bean bag chairs because of some random disease!

Now, there are some people who are born with, or who acquire, condition(s) that cause them to be overweight or obese. But I'll tell you they're very, very rare. Yes, it's becoming more common today, but guess why? Because we're passing down poor genetics (and bad Habits) caused by improper diet and lack of exercise, thus making the problem worse. And here's the catch: Your poor diet and expanding waistline can *cause* disease. But eating poorly and neglecting exercise is not a disease any more than refusing to file your taxes is a "disease." We've greatly confused cause and effect when it comes to our health and disease.

One of the primary causes of obesity is our typical Western Diet, the impact of which I talk about in many of my other books. The Western Diet isn't based on the principles of good nutrition. It's based on the erroneous belief that eating is more of recreational activity than it is a means of nourishing our bodies. This is why so many people in the Western Civilization die of heart attacks, strokes, diabetes, and other obesity related diseases. But there is good news. Years of research now indicate that the effects of the Western Diet can, for the most part, be reversed. Studies have shown that people who've abandoned the Western Diet for a more traditional and natural diet will regain health and reduce their chances of suffering from the usual Western Diet-induced chronic diseases. You can be a part of this. It starts with decluttering your refrigerator and pantries of all the "food" that's literally killing your energy level and ability to remain active as you get older.

I know I just threw a lot of information at you outlining the problem. But *"Gee, Gary, what's the solution?"* Remember Principle *#5, Take Action Today and Every Day.* Combine that with Habit #1 and you've got an instant recipe for getting off your butt and getting your health in order.

INTEGRATING HABIT #3

Here is a list of simple Habits that you can incorporate to make your overall health one big Habit:

1. Schedule your time for working out and physical activity. If it is on the schedule of your day you are far more likely to do it. I would recommend doing your workouts at a specific time frame this will make it a Habit. For most working out before starting their workday (to include me for over twenty years) almost guarantees you will do it, and cuts out the ability for you to make excuses if done later.

2. Learn how to cook your own food (not donuts and crap—healthy food). This is critical people who prepare their own food are far healthier in general than those who do not. Not to mention, it is far cheaper than eating out, more on that in the next chapter.

3. Pick a day to prepare your meals for the entire workweek.

4. Find people with the same healthy mindset and goals as you. Working out in groups helps keep you motivated, and their good Habits will rub off on you.

5. Stop blaming others for your health problems.

6. Get seven to eight hours of sleep every night. This one is very, very critical!

7. Create a list of health goals for every year and pin them on your refrigerator.

8. Try and exercise outdoors as much as possible, and make them things you enjoy, such as bike riding, hiking, walking, etc.

9. If you are new to working out, take it slow in the beginning! It is shocking how few people do

something as simple as going for a walk on a regular basis.

By now, I think it is becoming clear that in order to develop life changing Habits, it takes a whole host of smaller Habits.. You're already starting to see how Habit #1 works together with this one. You'll see more of these connections as we move ahead. Especially in this next Habit…

5

HABIT 4 - HAVING FINANCIAL DISCIPLINE

Financial discipline is the second leg of the *Three-Legged Stool* I mentioned earlier. Simply put, to me, money equals **FREEDOM!** The more money you have, the more potential for freedom you have and the more freedom you have, the less money it takes to maintain that freedom. This makes the Habit of Financial Discipline essential to living The Simple Life, and to living in harmony with the principles in this book. Just think about how many people you know who have to suspend or deny their dreams because they can't (financially) afford to risk a cut in pay?

What I want to make clear is that financial discipline is more about developing Habits around how you treat the money you already have. Investing is also important, but that is putting the carriage before the horse. Most people are so deep into debt, worrying about investing is a pipe dream. Once you develop the proper financial discipline then you can worry about where to put all that extra cash you didn't have before. Making more money is also important too. But it's pointless until you start taking care of the money you already have. This is why financial discipline is more about managing the money you already have.

Only when you have that handled does it make sense to start figuring out how to increase your income.

It is no secret that most American's are miserable; stuck in the daily meat grinder of a long (and getting longer) workweek and wearing themselves out on the hamster wheel of consumption. They're like cogs in the wheel of a brutal machine; a machine that uses OUR hard work and creativity to enrich the corrupt people who control the machine that I call "The Grid."

Most people in America are living as mere components of The Grid. Most of the work they invest into building up their own life is used to fuel this machine and those who control it. But like any other machine, The Grid is governed by a basic set of rules. Those who understand these rules control the machinery of The Grid and benefit from the energy put forth by hard-working people like you and me. In other words, they use the rules of The Grid to move money out of our pockets and into theirs. This then allows them to force their own warped "principles" on the rest of us.

The ONLY way to escape this is to understand the rules of The Grid, and to turn them to our advantage. This means adopting your OWN set of "lighthouse principles" for managing your money and your life. That's the foundation of developing financial discipline.

WHAT DOES MONEY MEAN TO YOU?

I want to challenge you to rethink your beliefs about money and personal finances. Most people see money as a means of gaining power/influence, or for buying stuff. Politicians and big businesses see it as a means of achieving power or satisfying greed. The everyday consumer might see money as a means of filling the void of unhappiness with shiny objects. In this chapter, we will focus on what money should mean to people like you and me.

I will say this with the most emphasis as I possibly can—if you want to be financially free, you must change your *thinking* Habits when it comes to money and how it is made and managed. This is essential for integrating your daily actions with the positive Habits and principles in this book. As I said earlier money represents... FREEDOM! I personally see every penny I earn and save as an investment in my freedom; freedom to do the things I want to do, and to live the life I want to live. I challenge you to think about money the same way.

In today's world, money can either bring us great happiness or great misery. This is why you must change your thoughts about money. For example, what are your personal motives for wanting money? People often confuse the desire for, and the pursuit of money as a form of greed. I both agree and disagree with this thought process. As I have pointed out, money means freedom to me. This is why you must give it the same care and attention as you would give to anything else that brings you freedom. If your primary focus is earning more money at the expense of your aspirations for freedom and happiness, that's a problem. It's this impulse that has caused greed to overrun governments, companies, and even the average Jane and Joe.

Where did we get the idea that to be successful you must continue to earn more and more money? This is a backwards type of thinking. First, making more money almost always requires you to expend more time and energy. This means time to enjoy the things that ultimately make you happy. Why give up your personal freedom for money, when you were originally trying to make money so you could have more personal freedom? Second, as we earn more money, we almost always spend more. This means more debt, more crap in our houses, and more worries about how to keep up with it all.

HOW MISUSE OF MONEY MAKES YOU A SLAVE

Imagine you owe $100,000 in student loan debt. Add this on top of all your other expenses, and you'll need to earn more money than your expenses/debt to pay down your student loans. This debt stops you from going on vacations. It stops you from paying off other bills, etc. Every dollar you pay towards servicing your student loan debt is also one less dollar for investing in your future.

Of course, you could move up in your career, make more money, and pay more towards the debt. After some years of hard work, you might even pay off this debt. When this happens, you get instant access to more of your monthly income. This is as good as getting a sudden raise. So now, because you've eliminated the debt, you have more money to live your ideal lifestyle. This means more freedom to do the things you want to do. And the more monthly expenses you can eliminate the more *available* money you will have. When you look at it this way, getting rid of debt is just as good as getting a raise. So, instead of busting your butt to make more money, why not work on getting more access to the money you're already making?

The problem is, most people are so saddled with debt and other meaningless expenses, they're literally too "poor" to live the life they want. And yes, this even happens to people who are making good money. So if you feel restricted by a lack of money, believe me, you're not alone. But don't assume that it's because you don't have enough money. Instead, let's take an honest look at the financial Habits of most people in our country...

- Between 1995 and 2015, consumer debt has skyrocketed. From 2000 to 2017 it doubled to $3.7

trillion, which is in the neighborhood of $11,000 for every person in the United States.

- A GoBankingRates survey in 2016, conducted as three Google Consumer Surveys, each targeted one of three age groups: Millennials, Generation Xers, and Baby Boomers/Seniors. They found one in three people had $0 saved for retirement and 23% had less than $10,000 saved for retirement. That's 50% of Americans who have less than $10,000 saved for retirement!

- Another GoBankingRates survey in 2016, found that 69% of Americans have less than $1,000 in savings.

- As of late 2020 the United States Government is around $24 trillion dollars in debt—four times what it was in 2000. In case you're wondering how this affects you, think inflation, cost of living, etc.

- According to a 2018 article in Forbes Magazine, Social Security is already paying out more than it takes in and is on pace to run out of money in 16 years.

As I'm writing this, the United States government is piling on trillions of dollars in additional debt to deal with the economic impact of the Coronavirus shutdown. You might argue that this is necessary during a crisis. But that's the problem with debt, it magnifies every crisis by forcing you to sink yourself deeper into debt because you lack the financial means to deal with it responsibly. Everyone knows what happens when you keep pilling debt on top of debt. You eventually become a slave to the people who own that debt. Is it smart to put ourselves in a position where we're forced to choose between our freedom and our well-being?

The kicker—the federal government doesn't have the money they are doling out like drunken sailors, but they do have a money printing press. If you think this doesn't affect you, you are wrong! The federal government runs off of our tax dollars so guess who is going to be responsible for paying back all that funny money? US! So you can now stack on the federal governments continued addiction to debt to your own personal debt. I don't know about you, but I call bullshit and so should you.

More importantly, how can we expect more money to solve our problems while we're being this irresponsible with what we already have? And if you think this sounds judgmental just look around at the people you know. How many of them are chained to jobs they'd rather quit because of their pressing financial obligations? How many of them are just two or three paychecks away from financial disaster? Remember Habit #1. Just as with your personal health, your financial independence is YOUR responsibility. And in case you're feeling sorry for yourself about being "poor…"

Did you know that if you're making a little over $30,000 a year, you're in the top one-percent of income earners in the world? According to the Global Rich List, a website that brings awareness to worldwide income disparities, an income of $32,400 a year will allow you to make the cut. Did you know that if you live in a place where the minimum wage is $15 an hour, you could make $31,200 a year just by working 40 hours every week? By the world's standards, the poorest people in the United States are considered some of the richest people on the planet!

Obviously, we have a severe spending and savings problem in our country. We have it in government, and we have it in our own lives. This is not to incite panic or make you curl up in the corner mumbling incoherently sucking on your thumb. Remember Principle #1: *Knowledge is Power*. But sometimes, knowledge has to scare you into taking action. So, this is about recognizing the problem and putting together a solid plan. If debt and consumerism is killing your financial independence, admit it so that you can start pursuing freedom!

INTEGRATING HABIT #4

Now, let's check out some practices for making financial discipline a Habit...

1. You need to list all your expenses and compare them to your income twice a year. If you don't know where you are spending your money and how much you make it is impossible to be financially responsible/independent.
2. Stop buying things on credit. Payoff and get rid of all your credit cards. If you can't afford to pay for it with cash—you can't afford it period.
3. Start with a six-month emergency fund, then work your way up to a twelve-month emergency fund. This means you must tabulate your true monthly living expenses to correctly figure this out (see #1).
4. Buy the car that fits your lifestyle and pay cash—its main purpose is to get you from point A to point B.
5. Only finance your house for fifteen-years or less with at least twenty-percent down.
6. Treat your health as a long-term investment. It is far cheaper to be healthy long-term than it is to spend your life going to the doctor, not to mention you are far more productive healthy (think money earning potential) than unhealthy.
7. Always purchase your clothes on sale. I have a couple favorite companies mainly for outdoor gear, and I know what time of the year they have their blowout specials up to fifty-percent off. A simple way to find

sales—purchase winter gear at the end of winter, purchase summer clothes at the end of summer.

8. Never shop just because you are bored and never go shopping just for the sake of shopping. For example, I never go looking for clothes unless I'm looking for something specific that **I NEED**.

9. Invest part of your extra money at the end of the month into something that will grow your money (after you have established your one-year emergency fund).

This is not an all-encompassing list. So, if you're interested in taking this to the next level, I go into a great deal of detail on how to develop Habits to be financially free in my book *The Simple Life Guide To Financial Freedom*. In this book, I show how almost every American has the potential to be a millionaire if they just changed their spending Habits.

By now, we've covered four essential Habits for living The Simple Life. Now, let's talk about the Habit that will make ALL four of these first Habits easier to learn and master…

6

HABIT 5 - KEEPING IT SIMPLE

Because my company and this book series are called *The Simple Life* you should have seen this one coming. The goal of this book is to empower you to stop chasing shortcuts and to integrate your Habits with a simple set of time-tested principles—not an overly complex time-management system or BS self-help philosophy.

Here is the primary factor that you need to understand when it comes to living The Simple Life and making things simpler—simple doesn't necessarily mean easy. I hate to break this to people, but being a productive, positive, and happy human-being is hard-work. It's also a lifetime commitment! For some reason we have decided we want it all now, we want it fast, and we want it easy. If you think that this is a realistic way to live your life, I have a unicorn to sell you... one that poops healthy cupcakes and gold bars.

Here is the kicker—most of us who are all spun up and living a life of being overwhelmed mentally, physically and spiritually, are in most cases doing it to ourselves. We have fallen into the trap of believing that more and more equals happiness. We are influenced by the Gridmasters into believing that accumulating things and shiny empty objects equals happiness. I like to be a contrarian to the Gridmasters, by embracing the "addition by subtraction" mindset.

I think you will be surprised by some of the examples I give you that completely stress us out and clutter our lives on a constant basis. In most cases for absolutely no rational reason.

We must remember that not too long ago we were primarily hunter-gathers living in very small communities or tribes. Our lives were simple and revolved around two things:

1. Survival
2. Reproduction

Obviously, if you weren't alive you couldn't reproduce. Which means worrying about reproduction without focusing on survival first would be fruitless. This makes survival our deepest and most powerful biological motivation. If you think our advances in technology, economics, education and psychology have changed this, think again.

Our hunter-gatherer genetics have changed very little, yet our lives today are drastically different from the lives that made us develop those hard-wired ancestral traits. In that sense, we're almost like fish out of water. We're living in a world that's completely different than the one we're biologically wired to live in. Basically, our brains are wired for our prior simpler lives. Yet, we are trying to force them to perform in ways they were never designed for. To drive this point home, let me share what I think is the biggest reason we're living a far more complicated life than necessary.

WHY ACCESS TO UNLIMITED INFORMATION OVERCOMPLICATES OUR LIVES

In Principle *#1 Knowledge is Power*, I mentioned how we should not confuse knowledge with information. Today, we have access

to more information than at any time in history. You would
think that's a good thing. But it can also feel like an army of
field mice scurrying through your head. As I said earlier, our
brain's primary function is survival. Anything outside this is just
considered unimportant information taking up space in our
heads. From the moment we open our eyes in the morning,
we're literally bombarded with information, much of it is
completely unnecessary. So our brains have to prioritize infor-
mation as it comes. And the more information comes in, the
harder our brain has to work. Of course, prioritizing informa-
tion is a good thing. But not when your brain is in survival
mode. In this mode, we filter things according to two primor-
dial categories...

1. Threats
2. Opportunities

For example, haven't you noticed how divisive and irrational
political debates are on social media? This happens because our
minds are so full of information, and we're so stressed out that
we lack the "mental bandwidth" to listen carefully to ideas or
people whom we see as "threats." On top of this, we see many of
our conversations as another opportunity to be heard or to
"outdo" someone else. You can escape this "everything is either a
threat or an opportunity" mindset by freeing up more of your
mental energy so you can become a wise, thoughtful, and empa-
thetic person. This means dumping the assumption that having
more information and more sophisticated technology makes us
more advanced as people. It doesn't.

I'd like to give you an example of how things have changed,
in the area of access to information, from when I was a kid
growing up in the 70s to today.

First, according to Daniel Levitin, McGill University
psychology professor and author of *The Organized Mind:*

Thinking Straight in the Age of Information Overload: "We've created more information in the last ten-years than in all of human history before that." That's where we are right now. Swamped with information, and in the process of dumping more junk into the swamp every day.

Now, rewind just a few decades. I remember the day my dad brought home our first, and only for that matter, set of Funk & Wagnalls encyclopedias (this was before our trip to Poorville). I'm pretty sure my sister and I were doing our goofy childhood happy dance as my dad opened the box, I can still vividly recall first setting eyes on them. I remember the smell of those books to this day. In a short time, we had every one of those encyclopedias spread from one end to the other of my sister's bedroom. That's how big of an event this was, and how important that encyclopedia set was in my life.

These were our one and only research tools. We had no computers, internet, smart phones, or even CD's. And we were still listening to good old vinyl records! For a kid, this was the mother lode of information, all in one spot. I was so excited that the encyclopedias even had pictures! We lived in the sticks, so other kids in our area would come over to use them for book reports. Or, we would just go through them page by page to keep ourselves entertained for hours on end. Oh, how times have changed!

Now, I know what some of you might be saying...

"You poor soul, Gary, your generation was so uninformed back then. You old people are just having trouble adapting."

I would say the opposite: My sister and I learned a great deal of educational and interesting facts from those books. Most importantly we remembered a lot of those facts. Can you recall what you looked up on the internet just a couple of hours ago?

Probably not, because you were more than likely checking social media, scrolling through newsfeeds, and reading a lot of other information that had nothing to do with your original search. And during that time, you were probably exposed to hundreds of ads.

During an hour or so on the internet, you're probably exposed to more information—most of it useless and unrelated to your original search—than I would have come across from perusing those encyclopedias for the entire day. On top of this, my encyclopedias had no ads for penis enlargement pills, vaginal cream or a prescription drug that would give me chronic diarrhea or blindness as a side effect. My Funk and Wagnall's encyclopedias were just pure information and facts.

This reminds me of what the good old American poet T.S. Eliot said, long before we had computers:

"Where is the life we have lost in living? Where is the wisdom we have lost in knowledge? Where is the knowledge we have lost in information?"

I challenge anyone reading this to ask what the difference is between being well-informed and being truly wise. Information hasn't made us wiser. Today, I would argue that it's made many of us less so.

To finish my contrast between yesterday and today, here's a comparison list (not comprehensive, but an example) of the sources of information I had access to as a kid and what's available now…

YOUNG AND BRIGHT-EYED GARY

- Television (no cable, a whopping four channels)

- Radio (terrestrial only)
- Books, magazines, newspapers (print only)
- Oral communication
- Educational institutions (brick and mortar schools)

Some of the above things had advertising, but at a fraction of the rate of today. Can you recall some of those old commercials? I can:

"He likes it! Hey, Mikey!"

I threw that in for nostalgic reasons—forty-years later I still remember it. Can you remember the ad you saw on the internet five minutes ago? Probably not.

A LITTLE SLOWER AND CRANKIER GARY

- Television (cable, internet-based, satellite, access to hundreds of channels)
- Radio (terrestrial, internet, satellite)
- Books, magazines, newspapers (internet, digital, print, audio)
- Oral communication (maybe, if you're lucky)
- Educational institutions (internet, digital, print, audio, video, brick and mortar)
- Internet (general)
- Websites
- Blogs
- Vlogs
- Social media (increasing all the time)
- Smart phone
- Desktop computer
- Laptop

- Tablet
- Smart watch
- Health tracker

Today we're mercilessly advertised to on these platforms. On top of this, buildings, buses, cars, even educational institutions look like they're being sponsored by every Fortune 500 company in this country.

Not to mention that the more information and options we have access to, the harder it is for our brains to make decisions. Having scores of options to choose from also creates the subconscious impression that we should be able to find the perfect video, or blog, or article or book. And this often sends us on endless searches for the perfect piece of content. Think about the last time you were watching a video on YouTube and clicked away after a few seconds because you thought there was something better to watch somewhere else. Having more options to choose from doesn't mean your decision about what to watch, or to read, or to buy will even be a good one. It just clutters your brain and makes it harder to pick something and stick with it.

Are you starting to see why the Habit of keeping it simple is so important?

HOW TO INCREASE YOUR FOCUS BY NARROWING YOUR OPTIONS

We need to step back and reanalyze what's truly important to us. We need to decide what's critical for us to live free and happy. We need to ask ourselves what life, wisdom and knowledge WE have lost in all this damn information.

I have a very simple philosophy: Keep it simple and focus on the things that matter. Remember the Five Core Principles of this book. Most of them are based on simple and timeless wisdom, not gobs of extra information.

With all the information now available at our fingertips, it's easy to get distracted and stressed over things that have nothing to do with our freedom or happiness. Why do I care that Kim Kardashian got another butt-enhancing procedure, or that another shady politician just got prosecuted, or in many cases escaped prosecution for crimes you and I would certainly go to prison for? The next thing you know, you're in the comments section, wasting time and getting spun up emotionally in something that has no bearing on your life.

There's so much competition for your attention—whether it be news, social media, or the marketing of products you don't need—and if you **don't** make a concerted effort to turn off a great deal of this noise, you'll live in a constant tornado of self-imposed, unessential information addiction.

Even though, there are numerous things we allow to complicate our lives, I believe the above is the most prevalent for us today. Every decision we make is based upon information and analyzing that information to come to a conclusion. Simply put, the more unnecessary information we have the harder it is to make rational well thought out decisions... life becomes not so simple!

The amount and quality of information we allow to come into our lives will ultimately determine our fate on this planet. Bad information equals bad decisions, which can lead to a very bad life. Reverse this and the opposite tends to occur.

By the way, if you're worried that having access to less information will make you less well-informed, you're admitting that you need to work on your decision-making skills. Decisive people have simpler lives, but they are still adequately informed about the things that matter most. This is because they're masters of filtering out what doesn't matter. So, if you want to be well-informed, start limiting your exposure to information.

You'll soon realize that limiting and filtering the information you receive makes it easier to make decisions. Do you really need to spend hours on social media getting involved in political debates with people you do not know, and probably know nothing or very little about what they are talking about? I would say a definite no!

HOW LITTLE THINGS ADD UP TO BIG OVERWHELM

Up to now, we've talked about the impact of information on a macro level. But I want to show you how little things (micro) add up without you even knowing it.

As the single guy, I often visit my friend's houses, who are married with kids, which gives me direct insight to how the average American family lives. Most of the time it is pretty eye-opening seeing what they focus a great deal of their lives on. I will also add, a lot of my friends with families seem to be constantly running on a treadmill of stress and being overwhelmed.

When I stay at their houses, I usually stay in their guest room, which is designated for such an occasion. I'm always amazed at the amount of time and money that has been spent on a room that is not used on a regular basis. The first thing I always notice is the ridiculous amount of pillows on the bed and how everything looks so perfectly placed. There is wall art, nick-nacks—it looks like a room for a prince or princess. Oh, I know some of you are wondering where the heck I'm going with this... just be patient and you will understand in a moment.

Most would think what a great looking room it is, so pretty... right? I look at it a bit differently. I first think how much time and energy was spent searching for all those useless items. Why do I need fifteen pillows stacked to the sky? How much money was spent on all these useless items? All I need is a functional bed, a couple pillows and a place to put my stuff... that is it.

But we have been brain washed by The Gridmasters and by the Dogma of the "Cult of Clutter" to believe that we must impress our guests and show them just how refined and successful we are. In reality, we are cluttering up our lives and our minds and going broke in the process.

Here is another micro example to drive this point home even further.

How many of us spend ridiculous amounts of time and money fixating on the decorating of our homes? Almost every home I walk into is jammed packed full of items that I consider to be unnecessary. Little do-dads on the shelf over here, massive couch, love-seat, recliner, reading chair (even though there are usually no books to be found), TV the size of your car, not to mention a garage filled to the brim of similar overflow items. With those great cooking shows, people today seem to need the biggest kitchen possible, and spend thousands of dollars on high-end cooking appliances, pots and pans, recipe books and everything else under the sun. The irony?

We cook our own food in this country at the lowest rate in our history. In addition, we are the unhealthiest developed country in the world... by far! So, it appears all that time and money spent on our kitchens is going completely to waste.

Now, don't take this the wrong way, I'm not saying the inside of your house should look like a Buddhist temple. But do you really need all those items? What purpose do they serve? Couldn't the limited time you have on this planet be spent doing something more productive?

When you add this all up piece by piece are you starting to see how complicated we are making our lives... unnecessarily? Not to mention all these self-imposed macro and micro decisions cause us to complain about not having enough money or time in life.

INTEGRATING HABIT #5

If you want less stress, less indecisiveness, and more happiness, here are some things to start doing today...

1. Figure out what is important in your life, not what other people tell you is important.
2. Get rid of unnecessary physical items, go through a decluttering process twice a year.
3. Decide what friendships align with your life goals, make you a better person, and truly make you happy. Get rid of the time-vampires, and drama kings and queens in your life.
4. Prioritize everything in your life. What is important, what isn't... and focus on the important things.
5. Before you purchase a new item, make sure it is something you need, serves a purpose and you can afford without using credit.
6. Get organized—being organized makes life a lot easier, and it is easy to get organized if you are not surrounded by piles of unnecessary items.
7. Be as healthy as possible. Yes, this is redundant from earlier, but I can't emphasize enough how living with integrity starts with your health.
8. Don't focus on the past or things you cannot control, live for the now and enjoy the moment.
9. Don't compare yourself to others... they are usually never as happy and successful as they look or say they are.

If you're one of the millions overwhelmed by the lifestyle of the Cult of Clutter, I highly recommend my book *The Simple Life Guide To Decluttering Your Life*. Believe me, your life is probably more cluttered than you realize, and I'm betting that's the cause of ninety-percent of your stress. You'll see exactly what I mean when you read my decluttering book.

Whew! If you're feeling overwhelmed by now, go back and read the Five Simple Life Principles again. Remember, this is not about changing all these things all at once. It's about avoiding extremes, taking action each and every day, and remembering that something is better than nothing. Use the Five Simple Life Principles as your compass and the outcomes will take care of themselves.

7

HABIT 6 - WISHING THOSE AROUND YOU WELL

This is probably the biggest reason people don't live by sound principles. They're too damn busy competing with other people whom they feel either threatened by, or jealous of. In today's hyper-competitive society, we tend to forget that we once survived by working together, not against each other. But we are in a strange place at this moment of time. On one side we are told competition is good and builds character (which I tend to believe this). On the other hand, we are told that competition is bad and that everyone is special and deserves a trophy simply for showing up.

Personally, I do think competition makes you better. It gives you something to strive for. But that all changes when competition turns into envy, jealousy and wishing bad things upon other people. Ironically, it's often the "everyone deserves a trophy" people who are seething with jealousy over other people's accomplishments. During interviews I often say: *"I want everyone to be successful, the more successful everyone is the better it is for all of us and the happier we will all be."* That may be very woo-woo of me, but I firmly believe it to be true. This is why I've made this the sixth Habit of The Simple Life Philosophy.

Research, (March 2019) in the *Journal of Happiness Studies*, investigations into several strategies for lowering anxiety and boosting well-being found that merely wishing a person well may do wonders for our mood. The research goes on to further state:

"Those who wished others well (loving-kindness) had lower anxiety, greater happiness, greater empathy, and higher feelings of caring and connectedness than those in a control condition."

If people are failing and wishing other people to fail, how does that help anyone? But it appears there are a lot of people with that mindset today... I know this all too well, as I was one of them.

COMPARATITUS: THE GUARANTEED PATH TO UNHAPPINESS

One sure way to make sure you're never consistently happy is to compare yourself with other people. And I'm not just talking about people you think are doing better than you. In the author world we often call it "comparison syndrome" or "comparatitus." You ask almost any author why they became an author and you will almost always get the answer: *"I'm an avid reader and with some of the more popular books I read, I felt I could do better."* I kid you not, we all say this. I have done it, and all the authors I know have muttered the same words. Here is where the comparatitus comes in: Once we become authors, we start comparing ourselves to the most successful authors in our genre, and the following words will invariably come:

"Why are they so successful? I've read their books, and they suck!"

I would say that is not wishing someone well. I'd also say that it's normally not very genuine, since many people criticize others this way out of envy.

Humans are wired to compete and compare. It is a survival mechanism. In our hunter gatherer days, we didn't have the endless food and resources we have today. We had to compete against other tribes, and other animals, for these life-giving resources.

Now that we are in a world of good and plenty, the people who don't have what others have often resent people who are doing better than them. In most cases those successful people (I'm excluding politicians, unicorn big business' and people who are born with silver spoons up their butts) worked really hard to get to where they are in life. In nearly all cases, we didn't see all the hard work before they became successful—we just see the success. So, if we don't see the sacrifices, it had to be all luck, right? Otherwise, surely you would be where they are at as well, right?

If you think like this, you need to stop. I have found comparing yourself to others to be completely unproductive. It is a waste of energy and time. You should be using that energy and time working on what you can control... you!

TAKE IT FROM A FORMER "COMPETITION ADDICT"

Trust me, I had to learn the lesson of this chapter the hard way. I grew up playing competitive sports. I also spent a large part if my life in the military and federal law enforcement. Matter of fact, I was so highly competitive in sports, when I competed against someone, I didn't just want to beat them, I wanted to beat them so badly, they would quit and never play the sport ever again. Oh yeah, I'm dead serious! If I lost a game of HORSE, I would lose my shit. I would want to keep playing until I won, and I wasn't very pleasant until that happened. If I lost a highly competitive athletic event I would sulk and pontificate on it for days. I would even lose it when one of my favorite teams lost... what was I thinking!?

Needless to say, I lived in a highly competitive mindset up until the time I left the government. This ended up being a huge negative force when I decided to truly run my own business. I spent a huge part of my time comparing myself to others who were doing better than me. I could have been spending that time learning and making my business better. Here is a major point I must make—anyone just starting out in anything... sucks at it at first. Hell, there was a time when you sucked at pooping in the toilet instead of your pants. If you doubt this, just ask your parents. We all suck when we start learning something new. That is just the way it goes. Every great once in a while someone will be incredibly good at something out of the gate, but it is very rare. As a matter of fact, in the entrepreneur world, we call these people the "unicorns." You never, never want to compare yourself to a unicorn. Not to mention that people who you assume to be unicorns might very well be people who worked damn hard to develop a skill or personality trait. You never know. So don't compare yourself to others. Instead, use your energy to get your own shit together. The more you compete with others, the more your beliefs and behaviors will come to revolve around the goal of outdoing someone else, and the less energy you'll have for integrating your Habits with the principles in this book.

This is why, for me to succeed, I had to change my mindset. Instead of comparing myself to others, I decided to look up to the others who were ahead of me. Rather than just trying to "model" their behaviors, I started searching for the principles that drove them. When I started doing this, I started learning from their success. I think you can see how the over-competitive mindset is mired in negativity. But wishing others well is based on positive thinking and a commitment to personal growth. I will tell you, once I changed from my highly competitive mindset to a positive one, things definitely changed for the better. I have always had a very hard work ethic, but when you use that work ethic on something negative, not much good is going to come of it.

CHANGING YOUR MINDSET FROM COMPETITIVE TO COMPLIMENTARY

Now let's take a little different perspective on what we've covered in this chapter. It is well known that your attitude and success in life is directly related to the people you surround yourself with. If you surround yourself with losers, well you have a pretty good idea of what you will probably become. Plus, how can you elevate yourself if you are wishing everyone around you to fail and they are actually doing it? You can't. Instead, elevate yourself by surrounding yourself with the kind of positive successful people who you aspire to be.

I'm in the self-help world. So I'm often in a position where I'm helping people who are not at my level yet. But, I actually hope they become better than me at what I'm teaching them. After all, if they become better than me, I can learn from that, and that will make me better. Also, if someone I teach becomes better than me, that means I did a damn good job teaching them!

Most importantly, when you start wishing people around you success, you'll be surprised at how quickly you'll attract successful and confident people into your life.

Are you starting to see how wishing people well is a smart Habit? They succeed, and you succeed... what a deal!

INTEGRATING HABIT #6

So how do we change from the hyper-critical and competitive mindset to a positive and encouraging one? How do we make wishing others well a Habit?

1. Spend every day of your life trying to be a better person. This will automatically make you want people to succeed.
2. I talked about positive imprinting in the Five Simple Life Principles at the beginning of this book. When you start to compare yourself to someone doing better than you say this to yourself: "(name of person) is doing really well, they motivate me, how do I get to where they are at?" I kid you not, you continue to do this and it will re-wire those negative thoughts into positive ones.
3. Just like earlier you need to learn to empathize and put yourself in other people's shoes. You can't wish someone well if you don't truly understand their situation in life.
4. Happiness and positivity is contagious... so be the good vibes virus!
5. Treat competition as a way to get better at something, not to prove your dominance.
6. Send people who are important in your life a special note on occasion thanking them for being who they are.
7. Show gratitude to those who help you. None of us become successful 100 percent on our own.
8. Help people when you can, and don't expect anything in return.
9. Congratulate people when you see them succeed at

something. Especially if your initial response to the news is to be jealous of their recent win.

10. If you're going to compare yourself with someone, compare yourself with the person you were yesterday, or last year. If you constantly focus on being better than you were in the past, you'll stop worrying about how you compare with others and you'll start becoming a better person.

8

HABIT 7 - SLEEP FOR HEALTH AND SUCCESS

E arlier in this book, I quoted Vince Lombardi, who said:

"Fatigue makes cowards of us all."

Think about how hard it is to pursue your goals and live with integrity when you're unrested all the time. Yet, so many of us go through the day feeling tired. It's no wonder: In the past forty years, adult Americans have reduced the amount of time they sleep each night by two hours! A recent survey found that many people sleep less than six hours per night, yet most researchers agree that adults need seven to nine hours of nightly slumber.

Sleeping patterns appear to have some correlation to body weight—as sleep time decreases, average weight increases. In 1960, only one in nine adults was obese. In 2019, this statistic jumped to one in three.

Sleep difficulties visit seventy-percent of us at least a few nights per week. A short-lived bout of insomnia is generally nothing to worry about. However, chronic sleep deprivation is a bigger concern, since it can lead to weight gain, high blood pressure, lowered immunity and poor cognitive function.

Some useful sleep facts:

- **Learning and memory:** Sleep allows the brain to commit new information to memory through a process called memory consolidation. In studies, people who'd slept after learning a task did better on subsequent tests.
- **Metabolism and weight:** Chronic sleep deprivation may cause weight gain by affecting the way our bodies process and store carbohydrates, and by altering levels of hormones that regulate our appetite.
- **Safety:** Chronic fatigue can lead to daytime drowsiness and unintentional naps. Such episodes may cause falls and potentially deadly mishaps, such as medical errors, and air traffic and road accidents.
- **Mood:** Sleep loss may result in irritability, impatience, an inability to concentrate, and moodiness. Too little sleep can also leave you too tired to do the things you enjoy.
- **Cardiovascular health:** Serious sleep disorders have been linked to hypertension, increased levels of stress hormones, and irregular heart rhythms.
- **Disease:** Sleep deprivation alters immune function. This includes the activity of "killer" immune cells (the "soldiers" of your immune system that seek out and destroy threatening viruses and bacteria that have "invaded" your body). Good sleep Habits may also help fight cancer.

THE SIMPLE LIFE GUIDE TO SMALL HABITS FOR BIG CHANGE 109

I know with our busy schedules, families and other obligations, it's often difficult to get seven to nine hours of sleep per night. But sleep goes such a long way toward improving your health and body shape that I urge you to try, even if you can only add a little bit of time to your nightly rest. Besides, which is better? Being awake, alert, healthy, happy and fully productive for sixteen-hours of the day, or being stressed out, semi-productive, unhealthy and semi-happy during 18 hours of the day?

Before industrialized society existed, our activity and sleep patterns were very in tune with the cycles of the sun and our natural environment. Because of this long history, when light stimulates your skin or eyes, *regardless of the source*, your brain and hormonal system think its morning. Here's why that's a bigger deal than you might think...

WHAT ARE CIRCADIAN RHYTHMS?

Your natural or circadian rhythm is the "internal body clock" that regulates the roughly twenty-four-hour cycle of biological processes shared by animals and plants alike. In other words, it regulates our sleep schedule. If we were to follow our natural circadian rhythms, we would start winding down as the sun set and would be ready for sleep by around ten pm. Most physical repairs occur while sleeping between ten pm and two am. After two am, and until you wake up at sunlight, your body is more focused on psychogenic (mental) repair.

Understanding how your body reacts to light is critical. Especially in a day and age when we watch TV or play with smart phones in brightly lit rooms well past sundown. In response to this light, artificial or otherwise, your hormonal system releases the stress hormone cortisol. This happens because your body considers light to be a form of electromagnetic stress, and cortisol readies your body for activity and the start of the day. So your body is responding to your late night

TV watching the same way it would respond to you getting up early and getting ready for a busy day. And we wonder why we can't sleep at night!

Cortisol levels peak between six am and nine am, but at the end of the day when darkness falls, your cortisol levels are greatly reduced. At the same time, melatonin (a sleep-regulating hormone) is released, as are growth and repair hormones. The take-home message? Use light to wake up, and dim the lights (including smart phone, computer, and TV screens) well before you want to fall asleep. Otherwise you're literally telling your body to keep you awake and alert when you should be trying to relax and sleep.

Studies have shown that people who have chaotic, irregular sleep schedules tend to release excessive amounts of cortisol throughout the day. If you're one of them, you may consequently suffer from fatigue of the adrenal glands (which are responsible for "fight-or-flight" responses). Adrenal gland fatigue causes additional storage of stomach fat, thus contributing to obesity.

Alternatively, some of you may be concerned about oversleeping. To ensure you rise at a consistent time every morning, leave your window blinds open. This allows natural sunlight to enter your room, stimulating the production of cortisol and waking your body gradually and naturally. It's also a hell of a lot more pleasant than groping around in the dark for that ear-splitting alarm during your first few waking seconds. If you live in an urban setting where streetlights are on all night and can disturb the quality of your sleep, some of these tips might be impractical. Get thick curtains, or a night mask if you have to. Your mental and physical health is worth it.

Most importantly, consistency in your sleep patterns will ensure that you'll wake up at the same time in the mornings without having to rely on raw willpower. You can also buy a clock that gently wakes you by simulating the gradual increase in light created by the sunrise. Again, this is much more pleasant to wake to than a jarring alarm!

INTEGRATING HABIT #7

1. Reduce or eliminate your exposure to bright lights, such as fluorescent lights, for at least two hours before you go to bed.
2. Go to sleep by ten-thirty pm. This means you need to be in bed by ten pm to allow enough time to wind down and fall asleep.
3. Don't consume any products or drinks containing sugar, caffeine or nicotine after one pm. This will allow your body sufficient time to eliminate most or all of these non-sleep-friendly stimulants before you snooze.
4. Get some exercise every day. However, try not to exercise too close to bedtime. I recommend completing your workout at least two hours before going to sleep.
5. Make sure you've finished your last meal of the day at least three hours before you retire. A light supper will be easier to digest and keep you more comfortable as you prepare for sleep.
6. Make sure your room is as dark as possible during the night or wear a sleep mask if it's impossible to eliminate light from your bedroom.
7. To prevent sleep-disrupting bathroom visits, don't drink any liquids two hours before bedtime.
8. Try reading an inspirational book thirty to forty-five minutes before bedtime (no detective novels, however! Too much suspense).
9. Follow your body's natural rhythms. I know my body

won't go to sleep if it's not ready. If I force myself to try to sleep when I'm not yet tired, I just remain awake for longer than if I had stayed up until I was ready to fall asleep naturally.

Follow a regular sleep schedule. You should go to bed and wake up at the same time every day whenever possible. I aim to do this even on weekends and holidays, so I don't have to readjust my sleep cycle when the weekend or holiday is over. When I sleep on a consistent schedule, I have a noticeable boost in my everyday energy levels, and I experience fewer sleepless or restless nights.

You've probably heard the saying…

"Early to bed and early to rise makes a man healthy, wealthy, and wise…"

This is true. But how much priority do we give to the "early to bed" part of that saying? Most of us try to get up early, without having a regular bedtime… and we wonder why the hell we hate mornings! So, while you're working on this Habit, remember that having a regular bedtime is just as important as having a regular getting up time.

9

HABIT 8 - FOCUS ON ONE THING AT A TIME

I t's time to tip over another sacred cow belief. This one is about personal productivity and multitasking. Multitasking is NOT making you more efficient. It's actually doing the opposite, and I can prove it.

The human brain is designed to focus on one task at a time and then move to the next one. Any deviation from this is abnormal and counterproductive. I've made this argument over the years, while doing interviews regarding primal health and living. Again, we were hunter-gatherers not too long ago. We had three primary tasks: hunting food, gathering food, and trying not to be food for something else (survival). This means whether you were out hunting, or at home protecting the little ones, you definitely weren't multitasking. If you heard a rustle in the bushes, you were laser focused on that noise until you figured out what it was. If you were hunting, you were off to see if you could catch it. If you were watching over your little ones, you were getting them out of danger as quickly as possible. You wouldn't be harvesting nuts, building a shelter, and then hunting or protecting your family all at the same time. If so, you and your family wouldn't have survived.

Yet today, we assume that because our technology has made multitasking safer and easier that our brains are equipped to do it efficiently. Not so. I know, you're probably thinking my argument is way out of date. But there's a sneaky scientific reason we've fooled ourselves into thinking that multitasking is more efficient than focusing on one thing at once.

MIT neuroscientist Earl Miller mirrors my above thoughts, saying that our brains are *"not wired to multitask well... when people think they're multitasking, they're actually just switching from one task to another very rapidly. And every time they do, there's a cognitive cost."*

Think of this "cognitive cost" like changing lanes in the middle of a traffic jam. Ever been stuck in traffic that seemed to have been caused by nothing? You drive in gridlock bumper to bumper traffic for miles, then it just magically clears up? Many times, this is because too many people are changing lanes trying to find the "perfect path" through the traffic jam. The cause of the jam might already be out of the road. But the constant lane changing keeps the highway congested. It's the same thing when you're constantly "changing lanes" between different tasks. You're jamming up your neural circuits and burning up time with all that "lane changing." But what most people don't know is that the Habit of multitasking actually rewires your brain to make you dependent on the Habit. That's the same thing substance addiction does to your brain.

For example, studies have found that multi-tasking causes three critical hormones to be released: cortisol (a stress hormone), adrenaline (the fight-or-flight hormone) and dopamine (the feel-good hormone). Achieving tasks releases a dose of dopamine, so jumping back and forth between small tasks gives you a sense of euphoria (a quick fix), even though you're accomplishing very little. It's almost like getting a little piece of candy every time you switch tasks. In short, you become an addict to these "brain candy" dumps of dopamine, adrenaline and cortisol. This is what turns you into a wound-up multitasking addict. And, as with other addictions, it also makes you more likely to defend and rationalize the behavior. I bet I'll get at least a few emails with people arguing about how productive multitasking has made them.

Imagine sitting down to a healthy nutritious meal. Now, compare that with eating a piece of candy every ten minutes, just for the sugar high. Which do you think is better for your long-term health? Now equate that to multitasking and its impact on your mental health. Your brain likes the "sugar-high" of switching between tasks. But by the end of the day, or the week, you're stuck in a traffic jam of half-finished tasks, scattered thoughts, and lingering worries about what you still have to do or might have forgotten to do. Does this sound familiar?

THE POWER OF HAVING A SINGLE FOCUS

Earlier in this book, I said that simplicity is one of the secrets to integrating your Habits with the principles in this book. Having a single focus makes this much, much more practical. As an author who spends a lot of time working at a desk alone, I have firsthand knowledge of how deceptively unproductive multi-tasking can be. Writing books is hard. And it's almost impossible if you don't focus and dedicate your time purely to writing... well, at least while writing. If you ask most productive and successful authors how they do it, you'll surely be told that they dedicate uninterrupted time to writing, and usually have a very strict schedule for this purpose. There's no stopping to check social media, answer emails, or make phone calls—their time is 100 percent dedicated to writing and finishing the next project or book. In other words, writers don't have the luxury of feeding a multitasking addiction. If we don't get things done, we literally don't get paid!

This is rarely true when you work in an office. Office life gives you almost unlimited excuses to invite interruption and distraction into your life. But that doesn't mean you're being effective. It just means you're getting away with accomplishing less because you always *look* busier than you are. This might offend some people. But it's much easier to hide subtle days (or weeks) of ineffectiveness when you're working for a larger company. In fact, I bet that's why most people are stressed to the max while at work. Too much multitasking. Have you ever met that aspiring author who's been writing their first book for the last five years and it's still not finished? Well, I have a pretty good idea of why it's not finished and why it probably never will be. Most likely, they're a multitasking addict.

In order to quiet the noise and block out those little brain candy hormone fixes, you must learn how to prioritize tasks AND protect yourself from people who interrupt you on a whim. Trust me, you'll be far less stressed out and far more productive than you've ever been. And here's the best part: You'll also have a great deal more free time to do the things you want to do! In fact, if you've ever gone from working for someone else in an office, to working by yourself at home, you've probably been surprised at how short your workdays are compared to how much you get done. Again, this is because single focus beats multitasking every time.

Here's an example of what my day can look like (my days can vary greatly depending on projects), based upon single-tasking and ranking of importance:

- 5:30 AM Upon waking, the first thing I do is check my email. All emails that are time sensitive I respond to—the others are left for later in the day.
- 6:15 AM Reading time (a current book I'm reading).

- 7:00 AM Feed and walk my dog.
- 8:00 - 10:30 AM (to include errands and driving time) If it's Monday, Wednesday or Friday, I then go to the gym for an hour or so of cardio and resistance training. I also have a small gym at home and if it's an especially busy day I will work out at home (I'm actually working out at home more and more).
- 11:00 AM Have my first meal of the day. This is a moving target as I only eat when I'm hungry usually two meals a day—just one on days of very little physical activity. The earliest would be 11:00 AM but could be as late as 3:00 PM.
- 11:00 AM Work on projects for business or conduct any interviews I may have.
- 1:00 PM Spend two to three hours on current writing projects.
- 3:00 PM Check e-mail again and respond to any critical emails, or ones that I didn't respond to in the morning.
- 3:30 PM Start to wrap up the day and unplug.

You may think this seems like a long workday. But this also includes walking dog time, physical exercise and running errands. So, when I say "unplug" at the end of the day, I mean it. I'm not checking and responding to work emails until I doze off with my smartphone in my hand. I live a balanced life, because I focus on one thing at a time.

Also, remember the above is just an example… I do not live a "groundhog" lifestyle. My work schedule varies depending on what projects I'm focusing on.

Are you seeing how straightforward, simple and single-task-at-a-time my day is? Do you see any reason you can't come up with your own plan to manage your day?

IF YOU STILL DOUBT ME, TRY THIS EXPERIMENT:

If you're still not convinced, I invite you to try focusing on one thing at a time for the next ninety days and monitor two things…

1. How dramatically your stress goes down after your "multitasking withdrawal" phase is over.
2. How much more you get done, and how much less time it takes you to do it.

Sure, maybe you've got a few more people interrupting you than just your dogs. Maybe you have kids or a spouse who works at home too and constantly tries to talk to you. I fully understand this. But do you take your kids to the office with you in a nine-to-five job? I would guess that is a big no. Nevertheless, I bet you've got a few "professional interrupters" at your office. But effective people don't let other people run their day. They know that managing interruptions is part of being productive and they work that into their plan. They also don't allow other people's "emergencies" to take precedent over their own priorities. Obviously, things come up and you may have to change the order of importance or add or delete a task. But if you have a plan, dealing with diversions will be much easier than if you're just flying by the seat of your pants.

So, try this experiment for the next ninety days, and see for yourself how much happier and productive you become. My guess is, that'll fully convince you of the power of this Habit.

I'll tell you; I gave up multi-tasking about a decade ago, and I've accomplished more than I ever thought would be possible. I now focus on the things that are truly important and block out the rest. I spend very little, if any, time on time-sucking distractions such as social media, clickbait news, random texting, or getting involved in other peoples' life dramas. Most importantly, when I'm working on a task or meeting with someone, I give that task or person my undivided attention. In other words, I don't interrupt myself while I'm working. More importantly, I try not to give people unfiltered twenty-four-seven access to me via phone, email, or text.

Some of you may also now see why I tell my followers that in order to contact me they must fill out the email form on my website. Filling out the form takes effort, not like social media where you can just say or ask something on a whim, expecting an instant response or answer. In addition, if you want updates from me, you must follow my blog or sign up to be a part of The Simple Life Insider's Circle. This allows me to more easily prioritize and accomplish the critical tasks for my business, thus making me more productive and giving me more free time. It also makes it easier to apply the previous Habit… getting a healthy night's sleep.

It's also worth mentioning that when you respond to someone right away, they don't always get your best response. When I was growing up, you didn't have instant access to someone via text or social media. This meant, if you had something to say to someone, you had time to think about it, to consider how to say it or whether you even should say it. Today, we have the opportunity to give someone our most immediate reaction. And that reaction is almost never our best reaction. If you doubt this, just look at how fast arguments escalate into mudslinging matches on social media. Too little delay between the brain and the keyboard.

So, this Habit can also help you with Habit #2: Don't Be an Asshole.

INTEGRATING HABIT #8

Here are some Habit-forming tips for getting things done without distractions:

1. Create a short, concise to-do list for yourself every day. But don't do it right before bed, as it may make you focus on things you want to get done and interrupt your ability to fall asleep.

2. Don't multi-task. Most multi-tasking is caused by shifting back and forth between things that are non-essential: e-mail, social media, texting... you get the point.

3. Get your news in a small ten-minute dose in the morning. If negative news puts you in a bad state of mind, move that ten-minute window to after your workday.

4. Take a break every couple of hours and clear your mind.

5. Exercise with no distractions. Focus on the task at hand and don't listen to current event podcasts or anything that's going to add unnecessary stress to your life. The point of exercise is to get and to stay in shape and to decompress. Not to jam more crap into your day.

6. Turn off any "interruption devices" while you're working on a project or connecting with someone in person. Even the most iron-clad will can't resist picking up the phone when it's right there on your desk and the text or email alert chime is on. Turn it off. Better yet, leave it in another room until you're done working on your project.

7. Stop bullshitting yourself about multitasking. Addicts tend to rationalize their behavior by explaining why it's good for them. This is just your brain protecting its multitasking addiction. Learn to recognize when you're telling yourself (or others) these stories, and recognize them for what they are: excuses.

8. Measure your productivity during your ninety-day

"no multitasking" experiment. It's easy to fool yourself about how effective (or ineffective) you're being. But if you keep track of how productive you are, you'll give yourself positive reinforcement to focus on one thing at a time.

This Habit will also help you accomplish the next Habit, which is one Habit in this book that will really turn your life around.

10

HABIT 9 - LIVE IN THE PRESENT, NOT IN THE PAST

During a large part of my life, it could be said I was wound a little tight. Not to say I didn't know how to have fun, but I definitely took many things in my life way too seriously. In my thirties, I started to realize I had the signs of obsessive compulsiveness. Meaning, once I locked onto something— usually in the form of projects, goals, or mistakes I had made in my life—I would continually obsess over them, literally driving myself nuts. From a very young age, I had a very difficult time sleeping. Thoughts were always running through my head...

"Why did we lose that game?"
"What could I have done better?"
"Am I ready for my algebra test tomorrow?"

On and on and on...

In both my youth, and my adulthood, these obsessive thoughts would keep me awake nearly every night. In short, I was constantly worried about things. In many cases, these thoughts were completely out of my control. I spent a large part of my early life physically and mentally exhausted. That is, until I recognized that I was the cause of this problem and that I needed to change my mindset, before I drove myself mad.

I recognized the brutal impact my obsessing had on my health after buying my first property—a condominium in San Diego, California. I was in my late twenties, so this investment was a big deal at the time. It was a fixer upper, and I wanted to do the remodeling work all on my own. So I started purchasing Do-It-Yourself books on basic electrical, plumbing, and remodeling. As with any project at this time in my life, I was fully consumed by it. I naturally have a busy mind, so if I don't have anything to do, I will find something to do just to fill the time. Sounds good on the surface. But there has to be a balance, which I learned later.

I was also employed as a Special Agent with the U.S. State Department Diplomatic Security Service. For those unfamiliar, that's probably the most grueling Special Agent job in the federal government. I was on the road traveling world-wide working long hours. I often worked several weeks without a day off. The job alone was more than enough to fill my daily stress bucket. Looking back, I have no idea why I thought remodeling my condo was a good idea at this same time. I chalk it up to the exuberance and naïveté of youth. But back then, I didn't know any better.

I remember getting home from a trip throwing my luggage on the floor and diving right back into my remodeling project without even eating or taking a shower. I would work hours and hours straight on the project, get a couple hours of sleep (if I was lucky), go to work, and repeat. I did this for several months until the remodeling project done.

I'm not a half-asser either. So, for my first remodeling project, it came out really well. As a matter of fact, a couple of the trades people I hired for the job asked if I was interested in working for *them*.

But I do remember once I was finished, that I just didn't feel right. Sure, I was proud of what I had accomplished. But something in my brain told me how I was going about things in my life (constantly obsessed) was slowly digging me an early grave. Not only that, I realized I had lost a great deal of what made me —me. I had always been a fun and outgoing guy growing up. But that was always balanced with a hyper-serious-focused side, which was very goal driven. I found that I was just too damn serious most of the time and that I really wasn't enjoying myself. I remember sitting in my living room staring at one of my perfectly painted walls—a job which probably took three-times as long as it should have, and decided that I needed to change something before my obsessiveness got out of control. Little did I know, this would be the start of my journey to what I now call The Simple Life.

HOW PRINCIPLE #1 STARTED MY SIMPLE LIFE JOURNEY

I'm not going to lie, I did some very deep soul searching and introspection before concluding that if I didn't change things, the rest of my life would be very unpleasant. I was always an avid reader, so I started where I always had when I wanted to learn something new… I started with books. I still had a copy of *Stephen Covey's, The 7 Habits of Highly Effective People*. That was required reading in my undergraduate college days. I can't remember what class it was for, but I want to thank that college professor for having the forethought to make a bunch of gooey brained college kids read it. I know it changed my life. What made this so amazing, was that the book was brand new, just released. I'm guessing it must have had a pretty profound effect on my college professor as well. I have probably gone through ten copies of this book over the years. In some cases, by losing it. In others, by letting people borrow and never having them return it. But I always bought another copy of Covey's book immediately. That is how important this book has become in my life.

As a matter of fact, there are two self-help/motivational books I believe everyone should read: *The 7 Habits of Highly Effective People* (mentioned above) and *The War of Art* by Stephen Pressfield. Remember those False Prophets I mentioned earlier in this book? The authors of these two books are NOT two of them. They're the real deal. Or, as I like to call them, the "Torch-bearers." These authors know what they are talking about and you should follow them! We'll get more into the difference between them and the False Prophets in the next chapter.

I started digging into what was making me unhappy and feeling unfulfilled. I found another thing that was causing me mental strife—by thirty years old I, had accomplished all the goals I had set out for myself in my teens and twenties. Still, I was floundering on what I was supposed to do next. I just wasn't prepared for answering that question. Of course, my obsessiveness was good in one sense. It made me work really hard and get things done. But at what cost? I was starting to feel I had wasted some of my younger years pursuing these goals... for what? I was still unhappy. Even though I had done everything society had told me, it wasn't working. Matter of fact, my obsession was having the opposite effect. It was making me unhappy and unfulfilled.

This was the beginning of my enlightenment. It's when I started realizing that life isn't about living the life others tell you you must live. It's about the life you really want to live. Who created these rules? Who created this belief anyway? All I know it wasn't me. Today, I have developed a philosophy about finding your own path in life and pursuing your own personal definition of freedom:

"Freedom is the ability to live a life in harmony with your highest principles without interfering with other people's rights to do the same."

Today, I feel most of us are so overwhelmed by what society and other people believe is best for us, we have made ourselves unhappy and unfulfilled. We need to start saying:

"This is my life. And as long as I'm not harming anyone, who cares how I choose to spend my time on this planet?"

Now, some people will confuse the above for doing whatever the hell they want, regardless of how it affects others or whether it's productive or not. That is not what I'm saying. You still have to integrate your Habits with principles that will make you a better person and the world a better place. Sitting in your underwear playing video games probably isn't the best choice—regardless of how happy it makes you. But, who am I to tell you not to do that? I do think a lot of people fill their idle time with wasteful activities. But that is their choice to make, not mine. All I can do is write my books and share my philosophy on how to achieve happiness. It is up to others to decide what to do with that information.

This is another example of my not obsessing about things I cannot control. Sure, I could sit around stressing out about whether people take my advice or not. But I could also choose to do the best I can by sharing my knowledge and experiences and letting the chips fall where they may. I'm not saying we shouldn't strive to get better. But there is a point when you have done all you can do, and you just have to let the results happen naturally. Constantly worrying about outcomes which you have no power over is a waste of energy and time.

I know that was a long-winded way of getting to the meat of this chapter. But I think it is important to tell my story. Over the years, I have met a lot of people whose stories are similar. When they decide to disengage from societal norms, and pursue their own self-defined happiness, they have similar revelations.

So, what does living in the moment or "mindfulness" really mean? We hear this jargon thrown around all the time today. Mindfulness is another one of those False Prophets using buzz-words without really knowing what it means.

Simply put, mindfulness is living in the moment. It means not worrying about the things out of your control. What is in the past is in the past. Unless you have a time machine in your garage you can't change it. That aside, all you can do is learn from the past and move on. Same with worries about the future. No matter how specific your dreams are for the future, you can never DO anything in the future. Now is all you have.

Let's dig a little deeper with the above explanation: reality is subjective. Meaning, it is different for everyone. Everyone has their own self-perceived reality. Reality is in the moment—right now. I can't enjoy or change the past or future, I can only deal with the moment right now. Once this moment passes, it's done. I know this can sound a little "out there," but this is how we understand the relationship between time and reality. Neither space, nor time are ever static. They are always moving forward, not backward.

HOW TO MAKE YOUR LIFE MORE ABOUT THE PRESENT

So, why would we spend so much time worrying about things we cannot change or which have no impact on our lives? Such an example is our political strife in this country today. How much time do people waste on political views or ideologies which they cannot control, and which have no impact on their life? The one thing you can control is your life, and your decisions in the right here and the right now.

We are very fortunate in this country. We have the freedom

to exercise Free Will. We can choose our direction and destiny in life. True, the Gridmasters don't make this easy. But, I never said that living with integrity was easy, it's just simpler. But we have the power to expand these options through making difference choices. Choices which are guided by our own internal wisdom of who we are, and what our life is about. There are many people in this world who have very little choice about their general lot in life because of where they live. Their destiny has already been chosen for them. If you're living in the United States, you have far more options than people in many other countries in this world.

But taking advantage of these options starts with understanding that the Gridmasters want you to think they are in control and that you have no choice. This is how they get you to live the life they want instead of you living the life *you* want. By living in the moment and changing the things, which are within your power to change, you take control away from the Gridmasters. They don't like this one bit, and that's why they aggressively guard their reputations as "experts."

THAT is what it means to be mindful. Living in the moment, and by your own internal values and aspirations. That is, assuming that those values and aspirations are yours and not someone else's.

According to an article in *Psychology Today* (June 2016): "*Mindful people are happier, more exuberant, more empathetic, and more secure. They have higher self-esteem and are more accepting of their own weaknesses. Anchoring awareness in the here and now reduces the kinds of impulsivity and reactivity that underlie depression, binge eating, and attention problems. Mindful people can hear negative feedback without feeling threatened. They fight less with their romantic partners and are more accommodating and less defensive. As a result, mindful couples have more satisfying relationships.*"

That all sounds pretty good to me. How about you?

INTEGRATING HABIT #9

So, how do we get into the Habit of living in the moment and turning off all the wasteful distractions, which are hard-wired into our brains? Let's take a look below…

1. Focus on the things that you can change to make your life better. Don't worry about the things that are outside of your power of change.
2. Get your news in small doses ten minutes or less a day. Again, do not obsess on the negativity in the news, which has no impact on your life.
3. Learn to quiet your mind—meditate on a daily basis. This has worked wonders for me, and I have a very busy mind.
4. Live your life—don't worry about how others live theirs. You'll influence people more this way than you ever will being a busybody and trying to "manage" other people (see Habit #14 for more on this point).
5. Implement Simple Life Principle #4 Take action today and every day. Don't try to do so much in one day that you stress yourself out.
6. Fill your free time with positive activities and hobbies.
7. Be compassionate to others, remember when I discussed empathy earlier in this book? Read that chapter every day for a month If you must.
8. Don't multi-task. Focus on the task you are doing right now then move on to the next one.
9. Learn to be a better listener. Focus on what someone is trying to tell you, not what you want to hear.
10. Get outside in nature—listen to the natural sounds

and rhythms of life. This will help you accept the natural pace of things, instead of obsessing over instant results.

11. Learn to decompress—if you are feeling stressed take a moment and reflect on the positive things in your life.

12. Plan for the future, but do not agonize over it. Take it day by day and master these Habits. The outcomes will take care of themselves.

I hope you're starting to see by now that this Habit is one of the most important of all. Without this Habit, you'll never find the strength and the energy to focus on what really matters. This Habit is how you clear out all the mental debris standing between you and your dreams.

11

HABIT 10 - STOP FOLLOWING FALSE PROPHETS

Over the last ten years I have noticed something very interesting. In spite of having access to more information in the history of humankind, it appears we lack the will to find the right information to better our lives. We have loads of information to pick from, yet we struggle with separating the good from the bad. It appears that we are literally drowning in information but starving for true wisdom.

Having this easy access to information is not a bad thing. You can learn almost anything with a few simple clicks. There are now over six million digital books available on Amazon. But how many of those books claiming to change your life for the positive will actually help you do so? Just the sheer number of these new self-help "experts" tells us there is a lot of bad information out there. Information that's being passed around from author to author, with little or none of them applying it in their life to see whether it works. In other words, most of these authors haven't integrated their Habits with the things they write about. They're leaving that job to you and their other readers.

The question is, why are we becoming unhealthier (at an

alarming rate), further in debt, and less satisfied with our lives, while we have all this information at our fingertips? There are many factors, but one of the most surprising I have found is that we're getting information from people who either have no background, or who have very little experience in what they claim to be experts in. These people are what I like to call the "False Prophets." They are the ones espousing "Fake it until you make it." Ironically, many people who read these books never make it out of the "Fake it" stage, because they're applying untested theories. Let's have a look at a few sobering examples of how poorly these False Prophets are failing...

THE CREEPING DANGER OF BOGUS SELF-HELP "EXPERTS"

The health world has always been a goldmine for False Prophets promising to cure all your ills. They promise fast weight-loss, or that you can become super ripped by just following their five minute a day exercise program, taking some magic weight-loss pill, or going on a diet where all you eat is papaya and coconuts. Anybody remember those magic health elixirs in the late 1800s laced with cocaine and heroin? Yes, I'm serious. Look it up. Or, look up the old cigarette commercials where doctors were promoting smoking as being good for your health.

False Prophets are not new. Unfortunately, people don't seem any better at seeing through their nonsense.

I noticed this trend of following False Prophets pick up steam when I started my primal health and lifestyle business. This was almost a decade ago. Today, False Prophets are crawling all over the self-help world like ants on a picnic basket. They look at you as a sucker, and an easy way to make money with very little effort.

But, when I first discovered them, the ancestral health movement was making another resurgence (when it comes to health fads, they go through cycles over and over it appears). I was, and still am a big fan of natural health, but I was noticing a lot of bloggers posting recipes and health advice that literally had zero background in health. One thing they did have was a big social media following and a ton of affiliate links. In case you're unfamiliar, affiliate links are promotional links leading to products which the website owner doesn't own, but which they earn a commission for promoting. Ever notice how you search for an honest review of a product, and you find an article from someone who "used it and loved it..." then they give you a link to click so you can buy the product? They're getting paid for any sales that come through that link.

Now there is nothing wrong with using affiliate links, but when your entire business and income is based on them that is a big problem.

In fact, one of my friends who has been ghostwriting online content since 2009 says that most of these "reviews" aren't even written by the person who owns the damn website. Instead, they pay a third world "writer" who has never used the product themselves to write a "review" about the product.

These False Prophets were using all kinds of other shady tactics to drive traffic to their websites and blogs and to promote products they themselves have never used. I kind of ignored them at first, but as I started getting more and more clients who were following these people, I noticed it was becoming a big problem. These False Prophets were pushing all kinds of dangerous supplements, weight-loss and general health advice. They have no clue what they were talking about, and again, many of them don't even write their own content. Shockingly, some of them were actually getting book publishing deals as health experts! I was truly flabbergasted.

The big problem I was having with my clients is they would find these False Prophets and destroy all the hard work we had done by experimenting with bullshit. Sometimes, I would get a new client who had already destroyed their health following one of these idiots. They'd spent all their money chasing false promises and had lost all faith in the natural health world. This meant I had to fix the damage these False Prophets had done. Needless to say, I was getting really pissed off!

But, remembering Principle #1, I decided to find out what had made my clients start following these chumps. So I started asking. Their answer was almost always that they had found or heard about them on social media… oh boy! Remember when word-of-mouth advertising used to be the most trusted way to find a good product or service? Social media has complicated that. It's now a haven for the False Prophets, and why not? It's a great place to pretend to be anything or anyone you want to be. Why people would get health advice from some social media darling puzzles me to say the least. But we are in a very strange place at this moment. Many people have still not learned how to recognize wolves in sheep's clothing while they're online.

After discovering how my clients were being led astray, I started digging into these supposed health experts. I investigated their backgrounds and it appeared that their entire experience was losing some weight (not keeping it off in most cases). That's literally all there was to it in many cases. They were an experiment of one… very scientifically valid (yes, that is sarcasm). No formal schooling, no courses, certificates… nothing, a big fat zero. Yet, scores of us are trusting our HEALTH to these chumps.

Have we lost our frigging minds!?

HOW COMMON ARE FALSE PROPHETS?

I would like to say they're pretty rare. But, that's simply not true. Probably the biggest surprise, was when I asked my clients if they had looked into the background of a supposed health expert. Almost all said no. Just think about how silly this is. We live in a society where we will spend countless hours researching that cute pair of shoes or seventy-inch TV, but zero time researching someone who could potentially kill us with their lack of knowledge or bad advice.

Of course, the False Prophets aren't only lurking in the shadows of the health industry. I use health as an example because it resonates big time with me, as it is the first leg of the Three-Legged Stool of living The Simple Life. But False Prophets are giving financial advice, business advice, relationship advice, and all kinds of other advice which they have little or no experience or education.

Why do we sabotage ourselves in this way? Could it be laziness, a lack of understanding what we are looking for, looking for the easiest way that placates us by telling us it is not necessary to put in the hard work?

Here is what I have found—and this is especially true when it comes to changing your health—by following someone who is not an expert in what they proscribe, it gives us an easy scapegoat. After all, if you are doing the hard work learning about basic health, nutrition, and exercise and following a well-respected expert (well-respected doesn't mean a big social media following) that puts failure or success directly on your shoulders. But if you follow someone who is not an expert, which usually means you're also not doing the additional research you should be doing on a topic—you can tell yourself that your failure isn't your fault! You simply move on to the next trendy False Prophet, and you soon have a life of perpetual failures that are not your fault.

In his book *The War of Art*, Stephen Pressfield calls this inner struggle "Resistance." In short, resistance is an obstacle to accomplishing your goals, and it starts with you. Resistance is always the result of taking the easy road... and the False Prophets are the tour guides of the easy road. If you want to change your life, you have to stop being a Self-Help Tourist, and start seeing these snake oil salesmen for what they are.

You need to find what I call the "Torchbearers" of the self-help world. These are the people/experts who do what they do because it is their calling. It is their life purpose—they would do it in some form no matter what even if they didn't get paid. Most importantly, they're not trying to sell you on some brand-new revolutionary secret that will produce results without work. Instead, Torchbearers pass the flame of timeless, practical wisdom from one person to another through their work. The False Prophets do it purely for money, greed and/or recognition. It is always about them and what they want. They love using shock and awe techniques, convincing you that you must have what they are selling, which is usually complete bullshit.

Some will put in a little work, by using some other experts work or material and calling it their own. You may be saying...

"Well as long as I get the right information who cares who I get it from?"

This is simply not logical thinking. It's just "Resistance" creeping into your mind again. In order to be successful at anything, you need the right information from the right people. This means people who have first-hand experience with what they're writing about. Otherwise, the person delivering the information will lose a LOT of insight while translating it into their own language. Many of them add their own ideas in, just to make it sound like they're being original. Other authors read and repackage these ideas, and that's how pure, untested rumors get into the self-help literature.

Why all the deception? Because the self-help industry generates eleven billion dollars a year. Yes, it appears our inability to get our act together is big business. Is it any wonder that a lot of self-help books are not written by the author whose name is on the cover? Yes, I'm serious. Most of those authors hire the writing out to someone else. Which means that health book you read last month might have been written by a forty-year-old, 356 lb man doing part-time writing work from his parent's basement. It's the old "widget in, widget out" mentality. All they want is your money.

INTEGRATING HABIT #10

So let's look at what we need to do in order to avoid these False Prophets:

1. You need to get into the mindset that you are the one who is ultimately responsible for your choices. If you don't change, nothing changes. The best advice on the planet is worthless if you don't use it.
2. Write down a list of the positive changes you want to make in your life. Then decide which ones you need to get help with and start researching the person(s) you want to get the information from. Starting with one authentic author beats reading from the "buffet of bullshit."
3. Avoid self-help advice from Hollywood celebrities. I worked on numerous diplomatic protection details at Hollywood functions. Yes, celebrities are rich and famous. But they have no real wisdom and are some of the most self-absorbed, clueless, greedy people on the planet. Besides, why would you get advice from someone who plays make-believe for a living?
4. Dig into the background first of the person you want to learn from or follow. Make sure they actually have knowledge and experience on the topic. Social media followings don't count. That might just represent how many people they've managed to fool.

5. Only follow people who do what they say. I have lost count of the supposed experts (a lot of them in the health industry) I have met in person who do none of the things they preach.

6. Real self-help authors are not here to be your friends. They are here to change your life. They are going to shake your inner core and beliefs at times, that is what real positive change is about. So stop being fooled by likable personalities, and start looking for real expertise.

7. Avoid any person promising quick and easy results. If it sounds too good to be true, it probably is.

8. Avoid going down multiple rabbit holes of change at once. I know people who have shelves and shelves of self-help books… that is a problem. Remember The Simple Life Principle's #2 Avoid Extremes and #3 Keep it Simple.

9. Don't be fooled by appearances. Between makeup, lighting tricks, Photoshop and advanced video editing, anyone can make themselves look richer and/or even healthier than they really are.

10. Figure out why you're vulnerable to False Prophets. What emotional need are you trying to meet, or compensate for, by falling for these people's bullshit? The more you know about your own "hot buttons," the harder it will be for hucksters to push them.

The good news is, the better you are at integrating the Habits in this book with the principles in this book, the better you'll get at seeing through the False Prophets. You'll also have more fun mastering this next Habit…

12

HABIT 11 - WALK TO THE BEAT OF YOUR OWN DRUM

I f there's one Habit that demonstrates personal integrity better than any in this book, it's this one. People with integrity don't follow the crowd. They walk to the beat of their own drummer.

Widget in, widget out, widget in, widget out... I feel today we have become "Widget Nation." What do I mean by this? I mean that it seems like our country, and world for that matter, run on the concept of working our butts off to make things, so that we can make money for buying more things. In other words, work to make widgets so that we can buy widgets from other people, so that they can have the money to buy more widgets from other people who are working to make widgets so they can buy widgets. Widget in, widget out. This model has very little creativity, freedom, fulfillment for those involved... it's just widget in, widget out—wash, rinse, repeat!

Today the creative or dynamic entrepreneur is looked at with puzzlement. Very few people understand why someone would do such a thing as to shoulder the risk of launching a new business venture. We have been taught that you need to go to school, get good grades, go to college, get married, have kids, get fat, go into massive debt, work until your body and mind give out, then if you are lucky, "retire" on a diet of dog food and Ensure while collecting a measly $1,000 a month check from the government. Sounds like a real dream, doesn't it? Why do we punish ourselves this way?

I don't think this is a dramatization of life today. The Grid-masters created this system and work really hard to keep it in place because it's how they get rich and maintain power. They do this because we voluntarily become a widget... their widget. Widgets are all the same—a means to an end. And it starts at a very young age...

"Don't buck the system little Johnny or you will be ridiculed and ostracized!"

I know this firsthand, as does anyone else who is even slightly awake. After I left the government a decade ago, I decided I was no longer going to belong to Widget Nation. The people around me thought I had lost my mind... literally! Try telling someone who lives in a place with high-rises, brutal traffic, soul sucking job with grinding hours, surrounded by hundreds of thousands of widgets that you are going to live free and off-the-grid. When I did this, they instantly thought I was going to disappear, live in a shack, eat squirrels and bugs, write a manifesto and surround myself with fifty-five gallon drums of rice and pancake batter. Anyone who has read the story of my adventure in my best-selling book *Going Off The Grid* knows this couldn't be further from the truth. Thanks to popular prepper and off the grid reality TV shows, which are in most cases completely fake—most people don't understand what off-grid living is really about.

WHEN CRAZY BECOMES SANE AND SANE BECOMES CRAZY

We live in the world where most people, in my opinion, have literally driven themselves nuts. When this happens, anyone who decides to take the sane path in life will be considered "crazy." Don't let this intimidate you. Today pursuing your own personal freedom and not being a "Widgeteer" is looked upon as some obtuse, esoteric type of lifestyle. Let that sink in for a moment. Living the life YOU want, not harming anyone, is considered abnormal today! In some cases, it's considered harmful or even dangerous to society. Is it any wonder why most kids today lack the ability to look another human being in the eye? Is it any wonder why some kids actually think strawberries come from the grocery store? This is not normal. It's just what's become popular. And the second you stop following this crowd, you should be honored if they consider you crazy.

Once I started on my journey of individualism and freedom, I came up with a saying when trying to explain my way of thinking to people:

"I'm so normal that people think I'm crazy."

Honestly, all I was doing back then was trying to be the best person I could be. I was living the life I wanted to live. I was trying to be a kinder, more in touch with nature, and a more self-reliant person. I was building a business that would put helping people first. All this while the majority of people were working to make widgets, so they would buy widgets, and more widgets, which would require them to work longer hours just to keep up with all their widgets. And yet, I was the weird one? Modern society's beliefs about what's normal have turned common sense on its head. Today, normal could be defined as "being and acting like everyone else." Yet, most people are unhappy, unfulfilled, and wandering through life aimlessly.

Makes perfect sense we would want to be just like everyone else… right? Huh! I call bullshit, and so should you.

BEING HAPPY STARTS WITH BEING YOURSELF

I consider following your own path and practicing individualism to be the spice of life. Different is good! I couldn't imagine spending my entire life doing what the Gridmasters wanted me to do—day after day—month after month—year after year. But guess what? That is exactly what we are doing. How many things do you do every-day because you were told that you were supposed to do them? How many of these things do you actually want to do? More importantly, how many of these things would you stop doing if you didn't believe you HAD to do them? Guess what? You don't! You can start being 100 percent happier right now, if you just stop doing what people think you should do, and start being yourself. So, why is this so damn hard to do?

Because to be the ultimate citizen, we are told we must be the ultimate consumer. Do you know that our economy is mostly based on consumerism? The majority of our economy and way of life is based upon us purchasing things, not on doing things. Well, the things you do (including that thankless job you spend forty-plus hours a week working) are all based on the widget in, widget out model. Consuming has nothing to do with happiness. Being your own person and doing things that make a difference has EVERYTHING to do with happiness.

Remember that Free Will thing I mentioned earlier? Here is the thing—if you like being a widget there is nothing wrong with that. I simply want you to understand that you don't have to feel trapped or forced to be a widget. You can use your Free Will to escape the soul-crushing machinery of The Grid. Is this harder than being a widget? Yes. But the rewards of not being a widget are unlimited. Anything worth doing takes work. Being different takes work. It's hard. It subjects you to criticism and even rejection from others. That is just the way it is. But if you never break the widget mold, you will never live the life you want. You will never enjoy that personal freedom you desire. Like I said, some people are completely content with the widget model, and that is their choice. Heck, you can even be a widget hybrid, or have what I like to call one foot in one foot out. But you should definitely ask yourself whether you're doing what you're doing because you really want to or not.

We have so many choices and freedoms in this country, but we have been brainwashed into thinking we do not. But the truth is, your level of freedom and happiness is within your control. You just need the courage to be... different. March to the beat of your own drum!

INTEGRATING HABIT #11

So what are some of the things you can do to embrace your inner goofball, and live a life true to yourself?

1. Start to realize that living the life you want is not abnormal, or something to be ridiculed. A lot of the people who thought I was losing my mind when I started now want to know how I did it!
2. Being different is about ignoring the noise and focusing on the things that truly matter in your life. If you listen to the noise, you will get derailed. In time, YOU will even become part of the noise by ridiculing people who are different. Don't be that person. Be your true self.
3. Create a list of things you're interested, in which, are considered abnormal or weird. Then, as long as the things on this list aren't hindering someone else's freedom, start doing these things!
4. Forget about looking "cool." For instance, I have

found one of the things that helped release me from the Widget Nation mindset was paying zero attention to fashion. Fashion is one of the main drivers of the Widget mindset and of the Cult of Clutter. I run my own business. I don't need to play dress-up to look "professional." Matter of fact, I don't own any dress clothes. I show up to meetings in my usual garb— cargo shorts, or a t-shirt. If it is cold, I wear jeans or cargo pants. Oh, I can hear the howling now *what a slob.*" Nope, that is my lifestyle and if you don't like it, we are not going to be doing business together. Wearing a suite and playing "good little widget" changes nothing. I'm the same person without it, only now I have more time and more money because I'm not wasting these things on portraying "the proper image."

5. Start deprogramming yourself from the Dogma of The Grid. People living in Widget Nation do many things Habitually—things that make absolutely no sense and some of which cause a great deal of harm. For instance, ordinary people are often amazed I do not eat on a schedule or three meals a day every day. But our eating Habits today, are based on the Consumer Nation philosophy, not on our genetics or health. I also do this crazy thing—I eat real food (you know that stuff that walks on and grows out of the ground) when I'm hungry. I eat at a different time every day. I don't do this just to be an oddball. I do it because I'm following what my body is telling me. A pretty crazy concept, right?

6. Don't belong to a "side," especially when it comes to politics. Analyze issues from all sides and make a rational well-thought out decision. The idea that you have to belong to a "team" is probably the biggest

deception of the Gridmasters. It's how they keep us fighting amongst ourselves while they run circles around us picking our pockets.

7. Learn to play an instrument or learn some other artistic skill. This will open your creative side, thus helping you think differently and more naturally.

8. Get in touch with nature. Nature is wildly unique and different—you just need to pay a little more attention to it... you will be amazed at what you see if you just start paying attention to the elegant balance in nature.

9. Kick controlling and negative people out of your life. Negative people typically want to keep you down so they don't have to feel inferior to you. This means, you'll do everything they can do to ridicule your plans to live your own life. These people are poison and should be avoided as such.

10. Start reading books you normally wouldn't read. Especially if you're worried about seeming weird or controversial for reading them. Following your own path in life doesn't have to mean you ignore other people's wisdom. Find people who have cut their own path in life, and read books by them, or about them. You might be surprised at how many of these "weird but successful" people you deeply identify with.

13

HABIT 12 - EMBRACE FAILURE

The saying "failure is not an option" is thrown around a lot in the motivational and self-help world. But I will tell you this with 100 percent certainty—you will fail in life—a lot! If you don't, that's a sure sign you're taking the safe path in life instead of the path to greatness. Here is a quote I like to use when teaching how to learn from failure:

"Your failures in life will not define you as a person, but how you react to those failures will!"

Today we are taught that everyone is special, everyone deserves a trophy, competition is bad, we need fluffy floors and Nerf corners, so you never get hurt or suffer. What a bunch of bullshit! Here is a fact: No one is born special. If anything makes you special, it's the choices you make and the risks you take while you're here. This will determine your lasting impact on others and on history—good or bad. Just "being here" doesn't do anything for anyone. You are not special for just breathing and taking up space. Humans are, just like any other life form, a grouping of organic biology. That is it. Sure, life itself is a miracle, and that makes your being here a miracle. But this has also happened trillions and trillions of times during the existence of our planet. The process may be considered "special," but you are just another small number in that equation. Again, if anything makes you special, it's the choices you make, and the risks you take.

Great things come from great failures and action--there cannot be success without failure. As we discussed earlier, whenever you learn something new you are going to start out sucking at it. Which means in order to get better, you must make mistakes and fail along the way. This also means that, by default, if you won't risk failure, you'll never accomplish much beyond just living an ordinary life. Once you get into that mindset, it opens an entire new realm of possibilities. It also erases your fear of failure. Instead, you see failure as a step in the growth process or a speed bump on the road to success.

FAMOUS PEOPLE WHO FAILED BIG

Did you know:

- Michael Jordan got cut from his high-school basketball team.
- Albert Einstein didn't start speaking until he was four, reading until he was seven, and was thought to be mentally handicapped.
- JK Rowling, the author of the Harry Potter series, was rejected by twelve publishers over several years before her manuscript was finally accepted.
- Walt Disney was once fired by a newspaper for his supposed "lack of imagination."

As a matter of fact, two world-renowned psychologists,

Daniel Kahneman and Amos Tversky, who won the Noble Prize for their work on why we are so averse to failure, did some research on this topic. What they found is that failures typically have a much bigger emotional impact upon us than our successes do—about twice as much to be exact. In other words, our failures aren't as bad as our reactions to them. So, you can change a lot about your life by changing your reactions to failure.

Look at it this way: the failures we go through while trying to reach a goal are the learning. The success, on the other hand, is the reward. In other words, the reward is not the lesson. The lessons lie in the failures we experience on the way to success. Have you ever noticed when you fail at something, you think and dwell on it much longer than you do when you achieve success? This is what separates the successful from the unsuccessful. Successful people work through and learn from their failures, while others give up.

We like to think of success as magic, or dumb luck, or being at the right place at the right time. Few people see it as the results of years and years of hard-work and failure leading up to the success. Yet, the second view is the correct one. Is it any wonder why so many people live ordinary lives?

TO FEAR FAILURE IS ULTIMATELY TO FEAR SUCCESS

I like to say…

"There is no problem, for which there is no solution, it is just a matter of how much pain you are willing to go through in order to solve the problem."

Here is one of the biggest things you must learn from failure; own it and move on. Don't make excuses or blame others (remember Habit #1). Admit your failure, figure out what you need to do about it, and fix it. Making excuses and blaming others is the easy way out. It takes far less energy than actually learning from your failure and solving the problem. If you continually blame others or make excuses, which I feel a lot of people are doing these days—it becomes a Habit... a very bad one. Pretty soon, you start to see it as the normal and logical, even the righteous thing to do. We are trying to develop good positive Habits, and blaming others is not the way to do it.

INTEGRATING HABIT #12

So let's put together the list of actions in order for you to conquer your fear of failure:

1. Realize you will fail and accept it. Every person who has achieved great success has had spectacular failures along the way. You will be no different. Expecting not to fail is setting yourself up for a big failure when you quit.

2. Anytime you start a new goal or positive changing venture in life, write down some of the possible failures you could experience during the process. This might sound negative, but anticipating possible failures will better prepare you for dealing with them if they do arise.

3. Remember that first leg of the three-legged stool for achieving The Simple Life—is achieving optimal health. When performing resistance training in order to build muscle, or even maintain it, you have to train to do what we call "training to failure." An example is when you perform a movement or exercise until you can no longer perform it. That is why people use a "spotter" while lifting weights. The spotter steps in so

you don't hurt yourself when you reach the "failure point." Not only does working out in this matter improve your health, but it mentally prepares you for failure in other things. So, start working out, and push yourself to the failure point. If you get into the Habit of reaching a physical failure point on a regular basis, you will have an easier time dealing with other kinds of failure.

4. Think of failure as a callus that gets harder and thickens with time. The more failure you overcome, the better you become at dealing with it. On the other hand, avoiding failure makes you soft and weak, and will make any failures very hard to deal with emotionally.

5. Never let someone convince you to not do something because you will fail. This happens all the time when someone wants to lose weight. Their inner circle tells them… "why even try you will not be able to stick with it?" Don't listen to these people. They're only expressing their own fear of failure by trying to make you afraid of it as well.

6. Again, surround yourself with positive successful people, and make sure some of them are more successful than you. They have already failed along the way, so you can learn what to avoid simply by knowing these people and talking to them. This doesn't mean you will not or will avoid failing yourself. It will, however, help you learn from other people's failures.

7. Never look at someone else's failures and assume that the same thing will "never happen to you." There's a fine line between optimism and denial, and assuming that you'll never fail will make failure that much harder to deal with. Instead, prepare yourself for what

you will do if you fail. Many times, this alone will lesson your fear of failure.

8. Have a "fail quota," and check yourself regularly to make sure you're not playing it too safe. In other words, if you're not occasionally failing at something, you're probably not growing or pursuing enough new things. Make it a Habit to do things which will make it possible for you to fail, to learn from your failures, and to get better.

The more you practice this Habit, the better you'll get at applying this next Habit and benefitting from it, which is closely related...

14

HABIT 13 - LEARN, LEARN, AND LEARN SOME MORE

I like to say: *"if you are not learning you are dead."* Now, I don't mean this literally, but figuratively. For me life would be pretty empty and boring without the continual process of learning. Simply put, you will never grow as a person unless you're continually bettering yourself or honing your skills by learning new things,

We are lucky today because we have so many opportunities to safely learn new things. Our not so distant ancestors had it much harder. They HAD to continue to learn in order to survive. Learning is the key to our two main hard-wired functions as a species—survival and reproduction. But for a long time, the ability to learn made the literal difference between life and death. Think of it this way—if our hunter-gather ancestors were incapable of learning, we wouldn't be here today. They would have just stayed in one spot and consumed everything until it ran out. Instead, they had to follow what animals had already learned—that you need to move to where the food is, and that means learning how to find the food, and how to safely travel to where it was. Not to mention that, animals, by their own learning process, eventually figure out that humans are dangerous to them, because we find them rather tasty! So, we also had to learn how to outsmart our food sources.

Through this learning process, humans eventually realized they could stay in one place by growing crops, and domesticating animals. Thus, greatly simplifying, and making their lives much less arduous. With that came less disease and longer life expectancy. So, through learning and progressing, we made survival and reproduction an easier process. More importantly, we freed up more of our time and energy for gathering other types of knowledge, writing it down, and passing it on to our descendants. In other words, the more we learned, the more we were able to learn.

Just as we learned to follow the food and to become an agrarian-based society, we learned that when times are hard and food is scarce, reproduction is not a wise choice. We learned that if we continued to reproduce during times of famine and drought, we would speed up our demise. So, by keeping our numbers down during rough times, we got better at long term survival.

Today, due to a great amount of prosperity in recent times, we no longer have to use learning as a survival mechanism. Because of this, we're less motivated to learn. However, failing to learn, still has dire consequences during our limited time on this planet. One such consequence is our loss of long-term happiness.

WHY MORE INFORMATION DOESN'T MEAN MORE LEARNING

According to the 2018 American Time Use study by the U.S. Bureau of Labor Statistics, Americans average around 16.5 minutes of reading for pleasure a day. Further analyses I conducted showed that Americans spend around seven-and-a-half hours a day on social media, the internet, playing video games, on our smart phone, and/or watching TV. These activities are becoming ingrained Habits, thus crowding out things, like reading, which is a good Habit.

Can we learn by doing the activities above? Yes. But it appears that we spend a great deal of our free time screwing off and making ourselves more stupid. The proof you may ask? Just like I said earlier, even though we are the most prosperous we have ever been, most of us are in debt up to our eyeballs, unhappy with our profession, depressed, and struggling just to get through every day. Considering how much information we have access to, it seems that the opposite should be true. Unfortunately, The False Prophets and Gridmasters are also using these opportunities to fill our heads with their own dogma about what it means to live a successful life.

This is the main goal of the Gridmasters and False Prophets: To keep us as stupid as possible, and make sure we rely upon them for everything we do. A perfect example is what used to be called the "USDA Food Pyramid."today it's called "the Food Plate," which is funny because it basically costed taxpayers two million dollars to change a triangle to a circle. But the original Food Pyramid was created for us by the USDA as a model for eating a healthy diet. So, after millions of years of evolutionary refinement, we are now the only animal on the planet that don't know what it's supposed to eat in order to survive and thrive? No other animal needs this kind of model to eat healthy. So, why should we believe that humans, being the most intelligent species, need a colorful, government-approved model to tell us how to eat healthy? The Gridmasters have done a fantastic job on that one. They've convinced us that we must rely on them for this information… and that we have to pay them to "research it."

The true irony is if you actually turn the food pyramid upside down, you have a better model of what a healthy diet would consist of. But, by not educating ourselves in the area of nutrition, and following the Food Pyramid blindly for decades, we have become the unhealthiest developed country in the world.

And guess who became filthy rich off what was portrayed as a healthy diet in the Food Pyramid? The healthcare industry. Food companies (mainly those selling processed foods). The sugar industry. The pharmaceutical industry. And, of course, our glorious U.S. Government got rich and powerful by collecting tax dollars from these industries. They've taken our money and been killing us in the process. Guess who the loser is? The uneducated public (you and me) who failed to take charge of their own health. Your health is your responsibility no one else's. All we need to do is this crazy thing called research and come to a rational conclusion. But, too many of us are dependent on The Gridmasters and False Prophets.

When I look at the Food Pyramid today, I actually laugh. That is how preposterous it is to me as a person who is highly informed on what a healthy diet truly consists of. To me, the Food Pyramid might as well be made with fairy dust. However, just a little over a decade ago, I was just like everyone else. That is, until I, due to numerous health problems, decided to take charge of my own health.

HOW THE GRIDMASTERS HIJACK OUR LEARNING INSTINCT

While learning is incredibly important, it's just as critical that you learn how to filter out and ignore bullshit information. But the catch is; the less you use that gooey mush in your head, the less likely you are to smell the bullshit when it presents itself. And it gets even worse. The less healthy you are, the harder it is for you to formulate and execute well thought out decisions. Are you starting to see how these bad Habits just keep piling and piling up and why the Habits in this book are so essential?

This is why I am always amazed when I see overweight people getting health advice from other overweight people or from people who have never been able to maintain a healthy lifestyle. This is like expecting to get sound financial advice from a personal finance advisor who is broke and has filed for bankruptcy multiple times. But guess what? People do this all the time. Today, finding a False Prophet has never been easier, because we put more time into researching and buying a new TV than we do developing critical positive life changing Habits. But, the more of these positive Habits you develop, the more personal evidence you'll have for weeding out horseshit.

I say this because our brains are actually wired to learn through a reward system. And the quality of your Habits determines whether that reward system works for your benefit, or for the benefit of the False Prophets.

We learn because of curiosity (a survival and learning mechanism) and because of a reward system hard-wired into our brain. This is good in one way as it shows that we're wired for learning. But, what are the Gridmasters and False Prophets doing? They're hijacking this hard-wired learning-reward system in our brains to get us to do what they want. In other words, they've conditioned us to blindly "learn" bad Habits. Why would anyone do this to us? Because they benefit from our Habits every time we pay them for more advice, more products, and more shiny useless widgets.

So, while we're wasting our time shopping for things we don't need—and in most cases we can't afford—and by chasing shiny objects, eating sugary nutrient-empty foods, the Gridmasters and False Prophets are making money by tapping into our learning and reward system. Our chemical reaction to learning is thus tricking our learning mechanism by short-circuiting it with the same chemical response we would get from learning good information.

We are literally becoming addicted to learning and repeating bad Habits!

The Gridmasters are, for the most part, treating us as lab

monkeys kept in a cage and controlled with "treats." Clever rats, aren't they? So, how do we make sure that our learning mechanism is working for us instead of against us?

HOW TO LINK LEARNING WITH REAL HAPPINESS

Let's go back to the Free Will concept. If we learn and turn positive actions into positive Habits, The Gridmasters can no longer trick us like lab monkeys. By continuously learning and being more self-reliant we gain the power to NOT be influenced by their negative controlling actions and propaganda. But if we're not learning on purpose, and if we're not making ourselves better and better, this will never happen, and the joke will continue to be on us.

INTEGRATING HABIT #13

Let's look at the best ways for us to turn learning into positive action:

1. Schedule in at least thirty minutes a day for *offline* reading. Reading upon itself is a learning mechanism. It helps to develop a larger vocabulary, exercises your mind and develops better communication skills to name a few.
2. Resist the False Prophets. Look into where you are getting your information and who is advising you. Do they have knowledge and experience in that field, or are they just fooling people with smart marketing gimmicks?
3. Pick a couple topics you are interested in and which will benefit you in life. Research these topics. Then take that information and implement it into changing your life for the better.

4. Learn by doing. Have you ever heard that saying: "book smart, but life stupid?" Putting what you learn into action is the key to becoming book smart AND life smart. Remember that failure thing? It is going to happen at some time no matter what. So remember *The Simple Life Principle #5 Take Action Today and Every Day.*

5. Remember that learning and changing your life for the better is your responsibility. Stop waiting for someone to do it for you. Do your own research. Even if someone has already done it and it's easier to simply read what they've written. Many times, doing your own research will show you just how full of crap a lot of supposed "experts" are.

6. Get your information in small to manageable chunks. Do you really need a 350-page book on the dangers of soy? Or an entire book series, whose main premise is to tell you to get up early and drink a glass of water when you first wake up? Many False Prophets dupe you by overwhelming you with tons of information on just a few key concepts. More isn't always better. That is why my books are always short and to the point. I want you to put what I teach into action... now!

7. Avoid social media as your primary source of information. And never treat it as a way of finding out what's "happening in the world." All you'll learn from social media is what's happening on social media. seventy-percent of all "fake news" is spread on social media. Only one-percent of all information spread on social media is considered original content—meaning ninety-nine-percent of it is shared, and not even created by the person sharing it.

8. Embrace your curiosity, because this is what being

human is all about. Today, our curiosity has been stifled because it eventually leads to us being free, and the Gridmasters don't want that. Follow your curiosity, even if it leads you down unconventional paths.

9. Treat learning as a tool for achieving freedom and happiness. The more you learn, the more potential you have to be free. Remember Principle #1: Knowledge is Power.

10. Take the time to learn about things that challenge your existing beliefs. A sure way to stunt your learning is to be rigid about what you THINK you "know." Many times, the best learning happens as a result of you challenging your own assumptions about the world.

11. Practice Habit #12 (Embrace Failure) by treating your "failures" as learning experiences. Successful people will tell you that they learned most of what they know, not from their successes, but from their failures.

Let me say one last thing about this Habit as it applies to the theme of this book. People who live with integrity are rare. Most people are so immersed in the "widget in, widget out" mindset, they have no definite principles to guide their Habits. Because of this, most of what you've learned from these people is probably only good for being just like them. The moment you part from this crowd and start following your own path, you'll need to unlearn what you've learned during your time in the Grid. More importantly, you'll have to replace that knowledge with knowing about how to follow the road less traveled without losing sight of your purpose and ending up back in The Grid. So, think of this Habit as your lifeline for living life by your standards instead of someone else's.

15

HABIT 14 - LET YOUR LIFE SPEAK FOR ITSELF

H ere we come to the Habit that leverages all the Habits in this book. Letting your life speak for itself is all about showing the world who you are instead of trying to convince them using clever arguments, social media, or other superficial status symbols. If your Habits are truly integrated with the principles of smart, simple and effective living, your life will be your most compelling message to the world.

You won't need to "prove" anything to anyone because your life will prove it for you.

Margaret Thatcher said…

"Being powerful is like being a lady. If you have to tell people you are, you aren't."

I would say the same thing about living with integrity. If you have to tell people what a good person you are, you're probably not very good. In fact, you might have noticed that people who brag about how honest or decent they are usually don't live up to their own words.

I think most things in life are like this. Good people are thought of as good because their lives show that they are good. Powerful and confident people command respect by their everyday actions. Smart people prove themselves out by the way they live, not by the way they talk. They don't have to brag about their academic or professional achievements or get into stupid arguments for the sake of proving someone else wrong.

Happy and successful people don't need to make a show of how rich, how loved, how sexy, or how respected they are. Most importantly, people with integrity don't have to tell you they have integrity, because their actions already reveal the truth. In other words, they let their lives speak for themselves. You should do the same.

Sadly, this is becoming a damn rare Habit for people to practice...

THE AGE OF VIRTUE-SIGNALING

There's no place where we neglect this Habit as much as we do on social media. Before the internet, only the rich, powerful and famous had the privilege of a public platform. Ordinary people could only watch from the sidelines wanting to be heard to matter. Today, we can all create our own personal platform where the entire world can hear what we have to say. This might be okay if we were better prepared to use it responsibly. But, when and how did people learn to do that? They didn't, and it really shows.

For example, watch people's social media profiles just after a tragic or controversial news story, like a mass shooting, a sexual assault allegation against a public figure, or a natural disaster. First, everyone changes their profile picture as if they're running some kind of commercial for what a nice person they are. Then their Facebook and Twitter accounts explode with posts about how horrible a certain public figure is, and why they should "resign in disgrace," or be fired, investigated, thrown in jail, dropped by their sponsors, or waterboarded with curdled milk. If the news is about someone's death, or multiple deaths, or someone being hurt or publicly humiliated, millions of people across social media act as if they'd personally known the victim(s).

Yes, people in pain need support. And sometimes people act like assholes and I'm 100 percent in favor of holding them accountable for it. But we should honestly ask ourselves how many of our social media rants, trolls, hashtags, memes, video reactions, or profile picture changes are just narcissistic virtue-signaling. If you think I'm being insensitive, or unreasonable, try this…

Next time you see a story about something bad happening to someone else, take twenty-five, fifty or one-hundred dollars out of your bank account and donate it to an organization that's actually trying to solve the problem that hurt that person. When you do this, DON'T advertise it on social media by saying…

"I just donated $100 to support…blah, blah, blah."

Just make the donation and don't tell anyone about it. Or, better yet, set aside a few hours during your weekend and go volunteer at one of these organizations. Again, don't brag about it on social media or call up your friends and "happen to mention" it during your conversation. Just do the volunteer work quietly and see how you feel about keeping it to yourself. If you can't, or won't, do this, or if you do it, but insist on advertising your good deeds on Twitter or Facebook, I question whether your motives are as pure as you say they are.

I think all of us could benefit from an honest self-examination about how much virtue-signaling we do in our everyday lives—not just on social media. Advertising your virtues does not make you a good person, nor does it fool anyone with half a brain into believing that you're a Saint. It does, however, feed your basic need to be seen, and to be heard, and to matter. My guess is, that's why so many people are addicted to virtue-signaling. It's not about the people they pretend to "stand with…" it's about their own attention-starved egos.

If you're not a virtue-signaler, good for you. But, there's another side to this "hey everyone, look at me" coin…

THE AGE OF DIGITAL DISSING

Let me be clear that I'm not one of these people who constantly accuses other people of "fat shaming," "slut shaming," or any of those other red letters some people like to paint on the rest of us. In fact, it's this type of public rebuking I want to talk about. Publicly dissing someone else might seem funny. You might think it makes you a hero. But I think we should all ask ourselves why we do this.

It's easy to shake your finger at someone who you think is a horrible person, or whose ideas you perceive as stupid, or dangerous. It's easy to accuse someone else of "gaslighting," or "covering" for a politician who you see as being crooked or corrupt. It's easy to shame someone for being pro-life, or pro-choice, for believing in gun-control, or for supporting the second amendment. It's easy to call someone else a "Climate Change Denier" or a "Useful Idiot" because they don't drink your preferred flavor of the political Kool-Aid. It's especially easy to do all these things when you're talking to a complete stranger over social media and you don't have to see the hurt on their face when you insult them. It's also easy to do this when you're in no danger of being punched in the face for acting like an asshat or for talking like you're ten feet tall and bulletproof when you're only 105 pounds soaking wet.

Again, living with integrity isn't about your words. It's about your consistent Habits. That's why I wrote this book.

It's easy to fool ourselves into believing that our view of the world is the right view. It takes real virtue, real compassion, and a lot of self-control to live by what you believe and to see the world through someone else's eyes. It takes courage to see someone you hotly disagree with as a human being who fears just as you do, who hopes just as you do, and who wants to be heard and valued just as you do. Yes, they may hope for different things than you do. They may fear different things than you do. They may draw validation from things which you see as dumb or insignificant. But for every person on your "side" of the argument who thinks this way, there's someone on the other side who thinks the same way about you and what you believe. Any chump can do that. It takes real wisdom to stand outside this crowd of finger pointers. Most of all, it takes integrity.

I think we can all benefit from deciding to see people with opposing political or religious views as simply seeing the world different than us. Yes, sometimes people are really, really wrong. What they believe might even be hurting other people. I demonstrated my agreement with this clearly when I talked about the False Prophets. But, for every False Prophet, every corrupt Politician, every sexual predator, and every mass murderer there's a million, or more, decent people who just want the same thing you and I want out of life: to be happy, to hope, and to matter.

Not to mention that many times, our accusations against another person are incorrect, and therefore turn the accused person into the real victim. I know this will piss some people off. But the truth is that not every public accusation is valid and we should investigate everything before we start clamoring for someone's life to be ruined. If we don't have time to do this, we should suspend our judgement and leave the job to the people who will take the time to gather all the facts and inform the rest of us. We should also remember that there was a time when people were burned at the stake, sawed in half, torn into pieces, and had their tongues cut out over accusations which were treated as undeniable evidence of real guilt. This was called the Dark Ages. It seems to me we should have outgrown that a long time ago. What do you think?

Finally, let me say that choosing to believe an accusation doesn't make you a champion of the victim. It makes you a reactive tool who supports the same tactics that forced millions of innocent people to suffer agonizing and publicly humiliating deaths over a period of hundreds of years in our history. If we're going to have social media in our world, we should use it as a people who are responsible enough to be worthy of inheriting such technology. Not as people who are stuck in the ignorance and superstition of an age we should have left behind long ago.

Again, letting your life speak for itself is what personal integrity is all about. Do this and you'll have less room for attacking other people on impulse.

"Gary, are you saying we should just sit by and do nothing about all the injustice in the world?"

Of course not. What I'm saying is that we should stop and do some real self-analysis into whether we're giving the world what it needs the most...

THE WORLD NEEDS ACTION, NOT TALK

Let's try an experiment. For the next year, say as little as possible about what you plan to do, or about what you think is wrong in the world, or about what you think someone else should do to solve society's problems.

Instead, write down a few simple things you plan to do to start mastering this Habit. First, write down your plans for getting your own shit together. You can't help anyone when your life is a mess. Next, make some simple plans for helping people who need your help and who, most importantly, who cannot possibly do anything for you in return. This second point is important because it eliminates the urge to help people for selfish motives.

You can also tell a lot about someone's integrity (or lack of it) by how they treat the people who can't help them or hurt them. So, if you want to show the world who you really are, find a way to help people who have no power to do anything back to you, for good or for ill. Follow this simple plan for a year, and I'll bet you two things will happen...

First, you'll learn a lot about your true motives. If you have to suppress the urge to brag about your plans or your accomplishments, to post about them on social media, or to tell everyone about all the good things you're doing, it means you have a virtue-signaling addiction. This experiment will show you that you can change it and become a person of genuine integrity.

The second thing that will happen, over time, is that you'll actually *become* a better person because you'll start to integrate your actions with the principles and Habits in this book. You'll realize that doing good for others carries its own internal rewards. It makes you more empathetic, patient, compassionate and understanding. Developing these traits is its own reward. Even if only you and a handful of people know how you did it.

Most importantly, this experiment will remind you of how shallow, stupid and short-sighted it is to look at everything from your point of view or to assume that people who have different values than you are bad or evil people. As you begin to realize this, you'll start to question your own beliefs with honesty. Your false or erroneous beliefs will be replaced by rational ones, and you'll remain open to the possibility that no matter how sure you feel of what you "know," you should always remember how easy it is to be wrong.

INTEGRATING HABIT #14

Here's a list of suggestions on how to go about this experiment...

1. Take a break from social media for six weeks. As you do, pay attention to your "withdrawal symptoms" and ask yourself what they reveal about you. Use this time to become consciousness of how addicted you've become to those positive (or negative) responses to your social media posts. You might be surprised at what an approval addict, or a troll, you've become.

2. Take a small amount of money and adopt a child in a third world country. Don't tell anyone about it. Don't post the child's picture on your refrigerator so all your friends will ask you who it is. Just do it for the sake of helping another human being have a better life.

3. Take a six-week break from political news. While you're on break, call up that friend of yours who has completely different political views than you do. My guess is, you've probably had a few fights with them over the past few years. Invite them to lunch and tell them you don't want to talk about politics. Instead, tell them you want to reconnect with them as a friend or family member. If you stay in touch with them after this, the topic of politics will probably come up. But, if you do this exercise, I'm betting the conversation will be a lot more civil.

4. Read at least one book a year (one a month if you read a lot) by an author whom you disagree with. Don't

read it with the intent of finding something wrong with their arguments. Just read it and ask yourself "what would I be like if I saw the world the way this person does?" If you know someone who agrees with the author, sit down and talk with them about the book after reading it. Ask them what they like about the author and try to understand their perspective before you argue with them about the book.

5. Read my book *The Simple Life - Life Balance Reboot* and get to work on your health, your finances and your life purpose. This is not just me trying to sell a book. If I knew of a better book for getting your entire life together one step at a time, I'd suggest that one. But I think you'll find this book the simplest and most practical road map to creating a life that speaks for itself.

6. If you have a disagreement with a close friend or family member on social media, talk to them about it in person instead of attacking them on social media. A lot of real world relationships get ruined in the fairy tale land of social media.

In closing, I want to share one final point about this Habit....

Make sure your life is actually *your* life and not a stand in for someone else's or for some fairy tale version of your life. A few weeks before I wrote this, the basketball player Kobe Bryant died in a helicopter accident. Very, very sad. Especially for the family he left behind. But I couldn't help but notice how many people were talking about him as if they'd just lost their best friend. In many cases, this is an example of people living vicariously through someone else.

Yes, I know. I spent a few pages talking about my heroes in the band Rush. I'm not saying we shouldn't be sad when we lose someone whom we consider a role model, whether we personally know them or not. But have you ever been to a funeral and seen someone who barely knew the deceased, crying their eyes out and getting hugs from everyone as if they'd just lost their best friend? This person isn't living their authentic life. They're trying to plug themselves into someone else's life.

This is mentally and emotionally unhealthy. Not to mention self-centered and narcissistic. The good news is, the more effort you put into getting your life together, the happier and more comfortable you'll feel, and the less need you'll feel to plug yourself into someone else's story. In time, you'll come to realize that your life can be pretty awesome if you just stop comparing yourself to others, stop looking for social validation, and start practicing the positive Habits in this book.

Actions speak louder than words. And no matter how you try to get around that rule, most people, including those with very little social intuition, can figure out who you really are just by watching you. Words alone will only fool gullible people and leave smart people questioning whether you are who you say you are. Be who you are. And let your life speak for itself.

16

INTEGRATING ALL THE SIMPLE LIFE HABITS

A s I said earlier, this book, and all the books in The Simple Life series for that matter, are based upon the information and guidance I wish I had thirty years ago. I don't write these books just to sell books, or cater to what people want to hear. I write these books to give people what I feel they need. Most importantly, I write these books to help all my readers give the world what it really needs. Right now, more than ever, the world needs people whose lives are examples of personal integrity.

That is a big difference between the Truth Prophets and the False Prophets. The False Prophets will write the books you want, in order to placate you, because they know you more-than-likely will not put in the hard work and truly make change for the better. Honestly, I could even sell even more books if I applied my knowledge of human nature to fooling people like that. But, that's just not who I am.

Most people today want the easy button, which never works long-term and the False Prophets know this. Widget in, widget out—give me your money! Hopefully, you now realize that The

Simple Life Philosophy is a refreshing alternative to this nonsense.

Integrating your actions with the life changing Habits and principles in this book takes work—today and for the remainder of your life. It never ends, and you should never want it to end. I have a saying:

"Expecting perfection from yourself and others is unrealistic, but pursuing perfection is a worthwhile endeavor."

That is at the heart of all the positive Habits in this book. They will never make you perfect, but they will make you better and better as time goes on. That is, if you continue to integrate them into your everyday behavior, which I believe you will.

I like to think of Habits as "continuous micro actions for achieving positive change." You know something is a Habit when you no longer have to think about it—when it just happens naturally and when needed. That's how you know you've integrated one of these Habits. For instance, people are amazed at how seriously I take my health in spite of how little I actually think about it. I know that sounds a bit strange. Especially to someone just getting started on a path of better health. But I have been doing this for so long now, I no longer think about it—at least not that much. I don't spend hours agonizing in the grocery store or writing out my workout routine day after day (I haven't done that in decades). I just wake up every morning knowing what needs to get done. Then, I do it. In other words, good health is easy now because I've formed the Habit of healthy living. Once something is ingrained, it is a Habit—long-term Habits become easier with time, but they are still hard-work to learn and master. This is why I've said, from the beginning, that integrity, simplicity, and peace of mind are all related. Once you've made it a Habit, living with integrity becomes incredibly simple. It's trying to keep up with the dogma of The Grid that drives people into worry and anxiety.

Life is about choices, and those choices—good or bad—are under your control. Sure, bad luck strikes from time to time. But if you form good Habits, and take control of your life, you can weather that bad luck... no problem. Matter of fact, there are some great lessons learned while dealing with those negative events that seem to come out of nowhere. Those who work hard and learn from "bad luck" develop those Habits. One of these Habits being the first Habit in this book "stop whining and blaming others" may be a struggle at times. But you will always come out the other side the better for it if you don't give up.

I will leave you with this. Remember that I didn't come up with the Habits in this book out of thin air. I feel these are the Habits that have benefitted me the most, and I have successfully taught them to many people over the years. These Habits also integrate well into The Five Simple Life Principles and The Simple Life Three-Legged Stool for Success, which I cover in other books. All of these books represent literally decades of trial and error and continuous work. Matter of fact, I still work on them today. Like I said the journey is never over, it just evolves as we get better. Most importantly, these Habits are all part of a well-integrated philosophy that will make anyone's life simpler and happier.

With that, I wish you great success in integrating these Habits, and in creating some more of your own. My goal is to help you live the life you want... so get out there and make it happen!

DID YOU ENJOY THIS BOOK? YOU CAN MAKE A BIG DIFFERENCE AND SPREAD THE WORD!

Reviews are the most powerful tool I have to bring attention to "The Simple Life." I'm an independently published author. Yes, I do a lot of this work myself. This helps me make sure the information I provide is straight from the heart and from my experiences, without some publishing company dictating what sells. You, the readers, are my muscle and marketing machine.

You're a committed group and a loyal bunch of fans!

I truly love my fans and the passion they have for my writing and products. Simply put, your reviews help bring more fans to my books and attention to what I'm trying to teach.

If you liked this book, or any of my others for that matter, I would be very grateful if you would spend a couple of minutes and leave a review. Doesn't have to be long, just something conveying your thoughts. If you would go to www.amazon.com and leave a review, it would be greatly appreciated.

If you hated this book, and think I suck, I would appreciate an email conveying your thoughts instead of writing a scathing review... that doesn't do either one of us any good.

Thank you!

Gary Collins

ABOUT GARY

Gary Collins has a very interesting and unique background that includes military intelligence, Special Agent for the U.S. State Department Diplomatic Security Service, U.S. Department of Health and Human Services, and U.S. Food and Drug Administration. Collins' background and expert knowledge brings a much-needed perspective to today's areas of simple living, health, nutrition, entrepreneurship, self-help and being more self-reliant. He holds an AS degree in Exercise Science, BS in Criminal Justice, and MS in Forensic Science.

Gary was raised in the High Desert at the basin of the Sierra Nevada mountain range in a rural part of California. He now lives off-the-grid part of the year in a remote area of NE Washington State, and the other part of year exploring in his travel trailer with his trusty black lab Barney.

He enjoyed and considers himself lucky to have grown up in a very small-town experiencing fishing, hunting, and anything outdoors from a very young age. He has been involved in organized sports, nutrition, and fitness for almost four decades. He is also an active follower and teacher of what he calls "life simplification." He often says:

"Today we're bombarded by too much stress, not enough time for personal fulfillment, and failing to take care of our health… there has to be a better way!"

In addition to being a best-selling author, he has taught at the University College level, consulted and trained college level athletes, and been interviewed for his expertise on various subjects by CBS Sports, Coast to Coast AM, The RT Network, and FOX News to name a few.

His website www.thesimplelifenow.com, Podcast "Your Better Life," and The Simple Life book series (his total lifestyle reboot), blows the lid off of conventional life and wellness expectations, and is considered essential for every person seeking a simpler, and happier life.

OTHER BOOKS BY GARY COLLINS

The Simple Life – Life Balance Reboot: The Three-Legged Stool for Health, Wealth and Purpose

The Simple Life Guide To Financial Freedom: Free Yourself from the Chains of Debt and Find Financial Peace

The Simple Life Guide To Decluttering Your Life: The How-To Book of Doing More with Less and Focusing on the Things That Matter

The Simple Life Guide To Optimal Health: How to Get Healthy and Feel Better Than Ever

The Simple Life Guide To RV Living: The Road to Freedom and The Mobile Lifestyle Revolution

The Beginners Guide To Living Off The Grid: The DIY Workbook for Living the Life You Want

Living Off The Grid: What to Expect While Living the Life of Ultimate Freedom and Tranquility

Going Off The Grid: The How-To Book of Simple Living and Happiness

Consulted and Co-Authored by Gary Collins - The Crime Beat Thriller Series by Best Selling Author AC Fuller

SOURCES

For a full list of references go to:

https://www.thesimplelifenow.com/habitsreferences

NOTES

NOTES